Cambridge Elements ≡

Elements in the Philosophy of Religion
edited by
Yujin Nagasawa
University of Birmingham

MIRACLES

David Basinger
Roberts Wesleyan College

CAMBRIDGE
UNIVERSITY PRESS

CAMBRIDGE
UNIVERSITY PRESS

University Printing House, Cambridge CB2 8BS, United Kingdom

One Liberty Plaza, 20th Floor, New York, NY 10006, USA

477 Williamstown Road, Port Melbourne, VIC 3207, Australia

314–321, 3rd Floor, Plot 3, Splendor Forum, Jasola District Centre,
New Delhi – 110025, India

79 Anson Road, #06–04/06, Singapore 079906

Cambridge University Press is part of the University of Cambridge.

It furthers the University's mission by disseminating knowledge in the pursuit of
education, learning, and research at the highest international levels of excellence.

www.cambridge.org
Information on this title: www.cambridge.org/9781108457460
DOI: 10.1017/9781108558167

First published 2018

A catalogue record for this publication is available from the British Library.

ISBN 978-1-108-45746-0 Paperback
ISSN 2399-5165 (online)
ISSN 2515-9763 (print)

Miracles

David Basinger

Abstract: *This Element is a critical overview of the manner in which the concept of miracle is understood and discussed in contemporary analytic philosophy of religion. In its most basic sense, a miracle is an unusual, unexpected, observable event brought about by direct divine intervention. The focus of this study is on the key conceptual, epistemological, and theological issues that this definition of the miraculous continues to raise. As this topic is of existential as well as theoretical interest to many, there is no reason to believe the concept of miracle won't continue to be of ongoing interest to philosophers.*

Keywords: *miracles, divine intervention, violations of natural laws*

ISSNs: 2399-5165 (online), 2515-9763 (print)
ISBNs: 9781108457460 (PB), 9781108558167 (OC)

1 Miracle Defined

A miracle, in its most general sense, is an event or development that is quite unusual and unexpected – from an unanticipated grade on an exam to the rediscovery of a hopelessly lost item of value to the rapid, welcomed change in how someone behaves. In its more restricted sense, the term is applied to those very unusual events that we would not have expected to occur given our current understanding of the relevant natural laws – events such as the emergence of a person totally unharmed from a horrific car accident in which everyone else died instantly or a person's immediate, total recovery from an end-stage terminal disease.

The focus of this Element, however, will be on religious miracles. Even at this point, some important initial distinctions are necessary. We need to distinguish among the ways in which the miraculous is defined by believers, the definitions mentioned tangentially in philosophical discussions, and the definition(s) around which most philosophical discussions are centered. While the ways in which believers identify miracles will be discussed throughout and tangential definitions will be briefly noted, the focus in this Section will be to identify the definition(s) of a religious miracle on which philosophical discussion in the analytic tradition has centered for at least the past fifty years.

Although specific definitions of a religious miracle differ greatly, the vast majority include at least the following two basic assumptions: that a miracle is an event that (1) is unusual in the sense that we would not have expected it to occur in the manner in which it did given our current understanding of how events occur and why; and (2) is in some manner the result of intentional divine activity.

Some have maintained that for an event to be labeled miraculous, it must also have a significant religious impact. For example, Robert Larmer (1988: 81) defines a miracle as "an extraordinary and *religiously significant physical event* [emphasis mine] that never would have occurred except through the relatively immediate action of a rational agent who, in some way, transcends nature." Timothy McGrew (2016: section 1.3) agrees:

> Beyond all of these considerations, one can make a case for the restriction of the term "miracle" to events that are supernaturally caused and have some *palpable religious significance* [emphasis mine]. An insignificant shift in a few grains of sand in the lonesome desert might, if it exceeded the productive powers of nature, qualify as a miracle in some thin sense, but it would manifestly lack religious significance and could not be used as the fulcrum for any interesting argument.

John Hick (1973: 51) also agrees, but makes explicit what Larmer and McGrew simply imply: that a miracle must be experienced by someone as having religious significance.

A miracle, whatever else it may be, is an event through which *we become vividly and immediately conscious of God as acting towards us*. A startling happening, even if it should involve a suspension of natural law, does not constitute for us a miracle in the religious sense of the word if it fails to make us intensely aware of God's presence. In order to be miraculous, an event must be *experienced as religiously significant* [emphasis added].

We need not read Hick as saying that only those who have themselves directly experienced the event in question can rightly label it miraculous. We can assume, I believe, that Hick would allow for indirect experience – for instance, the oral or written testimony of others – to be sufficient. However, the general point Hick, Larmer, and McGrew are making is clear. To rise to the level of a miracle, an event must at the very least be both experienced by someone and have a significant religious impact on this person. Or, stated differently, for those defining the miraculous this way, a necessary condition for considering an event miraculous is that it be an event that *points to* the divine for those experiencing it.

However, as David Corner (2017: section 9) notes, "if the question of whether an event is a miracle lies in its significance, and if its significance is a matter of how we understand it, then it is hard to see how the determination that some event is a miracle can avoid being an entirely subjective matter." While I'm not certain that including this experiential factor as a necessary condition renders the identification of a miracle entirely subjective, it does add significant subjectivity. Adding a certain amount of self-identified religious impact as a necessary condition for considering an event a miracle means, for instance, that there is nothing conceptually or epistemically problematic about two individuals – even if they hold identical beliefs about God's nature and how God interacts with humanity – disagreeing on whether a given event experienced by both should be considered miraculous. In fact, given this reading, an event considered miraculous by a given individual at one time might be deemed by this same individual to no longer be miraculous at another time if the religious significance originally experienced wanes.

Corner (2017, section 9) finds this problematic. Given this understanding of the miraculous:

> Whether or not a miracle has occurred depends on how the witnesses *see* it, and so (arguably) is more a fact about the witnesses, and their response to the event, than it is to the event itself. But we do not typically analyze human agency in this way; whether or not Caesar crossed the Rubicon is not a matter of how anyone experiences things. The question of whether Caesar crossed the Rubicon is an objective one. Surely the theist wishes to say that the question of whether God has acted in the world, in the occurrence of a miracle, is objective as well. And surely this fact accounts for the attractiveness of a causal account of miracles; any dispute over the cause of a putative miracle is a dispute over the facts, not a dispute about how people *view* the facts.

While I'm personally sympathetic to this concern, it is not the main reason I won't be incorporating any type of "experiencing as" component into the definition around which this study will focus. The reason, rather, is because most philosophical discussions of the miraculous haven't been concerned with how, or even if, any specific event considered miraculous has affected or would affect any given individual's psychological states. Rather, most discussions have focused on the relationship, in principle, between the event and the natural order and the relationship, in principle, between the event and divine causation. In the words of Morgan Luck (2016: 267), most miracle definitions have the same structure: that of a "natural effect (that is, an effect within space-time) with a non-natural cause." And we will follow suit.

It is also important at this point to clarify in what sense a miracle, as we are defining the term, must be observable. While many theists hold that some of their most personal, significant religious experiences – for example, an unexpected sense of peace after the painful loss of a loved one or freedom from feelings of long-standing anger and resentment – are the result of some form of compassionate divine intervention, in most philosophical discussions such experiences aren't categorized as miraculous. Rather, "miracle" is normally reserved for those unexpected, unusual events that are, in principle, observable to all as states of affairs that we would not have been expected to occur as they did given our understanding of the natural order.

It is also important to emphasize that it doesn't follow from this that only those events that have actually been observed can be candidates for a miracle. To say that a miracle is an event that is, *in principle*, observable is to say that it would or could be observed if there were individuals present to do so. Otherwise, we rule out what I believe most theists affirm and most philosophers accept: that an unusual event caused by God, but never actually detected, can still rightly qualify as a miracle. Stephen Evans (1985: 110), I believe, captures this well when he asks us to "suppose . . . that a crucial bolt on an airliner is about to fail, and that in response to prayer for the safekeeping of those on board God miraculously fuses the bolt," and then adds that "to all outward appearances the flight is uneventful; nevertheless the safe arrival of the plane is a miracle."

Before beginning our discussion of additional definitional clarifications related specifically to the miraculous as an event and then as an act of God, a final general observation is necessary.

This Element is not a survey of the way in which the miraculous is understood in the various world religions. The purpose of this Element is to update the discussion of a miracle as it has taken place within Western analytic philosophy. Within this context, the focus has normally been narrowed down to religious belief systems that posit a supernatural being (God) with the capacity to intervene in earthly affairs in ways that are contrary to our understanding of the natural order.

While much of my discussion (mirroring the discussion at large) will focus on the God of Christianity, it is important to note that variants of other religious traditions also posit the existence of a supernatural being who intervenes miraculously in our world. Judaism obviously fits into this category, as within the Torah (the first five books of the Christian Old Testament) examples of God intervening in ways that are contrary to the laws of nature abound. Moreover, within more orthodox strands of Judaism, belief in such divine interaction remains today (Jacobs, n.d.).

Likewise, within Islam, some define a miracle "as an extraordinary act or event that is contrary to the laws of nature and can only come about through the direct intervention of God Almighty Himself" or is "performed by the permission of God, by the Prophets of God" (Stacey, 2014).

While most within Hinduism focus on human mystics who can perform acts that defy natural explanation – for example, healing the sick or levitating – the Hindu scriptures also attribute interventive activity to the gods and goddesses (Kriger, n.d.).

Accordingly, while our focus will be primarily on miracles within a Christian context, it's important to note that the concerns/challenges we will be considering arise within any religious belief system that posits a supernatural being who can/does intervene intentionally in earthly affairs.

1.1   A Miracle as an Unusual Event

We will first consider only those definitional clarifications primarily related to the miraculous as an unusual event, with clarifications primarily related to the miraculous as an act of God to follow.

A miracle, given the definition with which we are working, is an event that is unusual in the sense that we would not have expected it to occur in the manner in which it did, given our current understanding of how events occur and why. There are, though, at least three distinct understandings of what it means to say that a miraculous event is unusual around which philosophical discussion have arisen, understandings that differ on the perceived relationship between a miraculous event, qua event, and the natural order.

1.1.1   A Miracle as a Violation of a Natural Law

At least since the time of David Hume, miracles have often been defined by proponents and critics alike as violations of natural laws.

While there is no noncontroversial understanding of what would constitute a violation of such laws, something like the following seems frequently to be intended by those who consider the concept coherent. Natural laws describe actual uniformities that occur in our world. More specifically, they are universal generalizations describing what will happen (or not) under specifiable conditions. Some of our best-established natural laws confirm for us, for instance, that water does not turn instantly into wine and that a floating body always displaces an amount of fluid the weight of which is equal to its own weight.

But let us assume that water actually did turn instantly into wine or that someone were to walk on water. We would then, it is argued, be required to acknowledge not only the occurrence of an event that our knowledge of natural laws gives us good reason to believe will not occur; more importantly, we would then be required to acknowledge the occurrence of an event for which we could justifiably conclude no natural explanation could ever be forthcoming. Accordingly, proponents of this line of reasoning conclude, we would be justified in assuming that the relevant natural laws had been violated (Drange, 1998).

As we will discuss in Section 2, many have challenged the coherence of this understanding of miracle. Also, as we will discuss in Sections 3 and 4, even if coherent, this concept of miracle raises epistemological and moral concerns.

1.1.2 A Miracle as an Overriding or Circumvention of a Natural Law

This understanding of the relationship between a miraculous event and the natural order focuses on the scope of the natural order vis-à-vis the occurrence in question. Specifically, it's based on the assumption that our current understanding of the natural order can only be challenged by occurrences that have, in principle, totally natural causal explanations and, thus, that an event that is in part the result of non-natural causation is best viewed as a circumvention (overriding) of the natural order rather than as a violation of this order.

For example, Steve Clarke (1997: 96), when discussing the relationship between miracle and natural law, tells us that "laws of nature are *of nature*; they should not be expected to account for the behavior of things which have been supernaturally interfered with." In a similar vein, Thomas Aquinas (SCG3) states that a miracle is an event that exceeds the productive power of nature.

Leigh Vicens (2016: 34), when expanding on Peter van Inwagen's views on divine action, offers us a unique version of this understanding of miracle tied to modern science:

> Suppose, then, that creation consists of a certain number of indivisible units of matter called "elementary particles," and that these particles possess certain causal powers – that is, certain intrinsic capacities to affect the motions of other particles. Suppose further that God created these particles out of nothing, and continually sustains their existence and conserves their powers. In such a world, a miracle could amount to this: God's occasionally, and momentarily, supplying some elementary particles with causal powers *different* from their normal ones. We might imagine, to use van Inwagen's example, that God makes the particles composing some water molecules follow different trajectories than they normally do, thus rearranging themselves into wine. If such a divine action counts as a miracle then, van Inwagen notes, a miracle is not necessarily a law violation ... [as long as]the laws of nature are indeterministic.

While not as controversial conceptually as violation miracles, the understanding of a miraculous event as a circumvention (or overriding) of nature is, as we will see, subject to the same types of epistemological and moral challenges.

1.1.3   A Miracle as a Coincidence with an Available Natural Explanation

Not all philosophers and theists believe, however, that "miracle" can be used to describe an event only when no plausible natural explanation is (or could be) available. Let's consider, for instance, the following, oft-repeated hypothetical story by R. F. Holland (1965). A child has ridden his toy motorcar onto an unguarded railway crossing near his house, and one of the wheels on his car gets stuck on one of the rails. An express train is approaching and a curve in the track makes it impossible for the driver to see the child. Moreover, the child is so intent on freeing his wheel that he doesn't hear the train whistle or his mother, who has come out of the house and is trying to get his attention. It appears the child is doomed. However, just before the train rounds the curve the brakes are applied, and the train stops just a few feet from the child. The mother immediately thanks God for what she considers a miracle, even though she comes to learn that there was not necessarily anything supernatural about the manner in which the train came to stop just short of her son. The driver had fainted for reasons unrelated to the presence of the child on the line, and the brakes were applied automatically when his hand released pressure on the control lever.

Every observable component in this event sequence has an available natural explanation. Children do sometimes play on train tracks; those driving trains sometimes faint; and the brakes of trains have been designed to become operative when the control lever is not engaged.

Holland himself used this story to exemplify what he labeled "coincidence" miracles – events that deserve to be called miracles not because they have no natural explanation or because God in some ways directly intervened but because of their unexpected but significant outcome. I want to use Holland's story to illustrate another way of understanding how God can intervene in the natural order. There are clearly many theists who understand miracles to be events that at least presently have no obvious fully natural explanation (and, hence, view such violations or circumventions of the natural order). It's also the case that no theist would deny that there are some very significant unexpected events, let's label them coincidences, that don't involve direct divine intervention at all. However, at least some theists also believe there to be significant unexpected events, which we will also label coincidences, with fully natural explanations available that do nevertheless involve direct divine intervention.

In the Holland story, as noted, a fully natural explanation is clearly present. However, another explanatory option is available in this situation: that the driver fainted at the precise moment because God directly intervened in some manner to make it so. And there are theists who would claim that if there was, in fact, direct divine intervention of this sort in this case then this event could justifiably be considered a miracle, even granting that a totally natural explanation would also be at hand. Other possible coincidence miracles of this sort might include a situation in which it is assumed that God brings to someone's mind an elderly relative and for that reason this person stops by the relative's home just in time to save her life by calling for emergency help, or a situation in which God brings it about that a person has a flat tire on the way to the airport and for this reason doesn't make it in time to board a plane that crashes.

To generalize the key point, there are theists (and philosophers) who do not want to limit the range of the term "miracle" to only those direct divine interventions for which no natural explanation is presently available. They want to expand the definition to cover those "coincidences" in relation to which God has directly manipu-lated the natural order, even though a plausible alternate fully natural causal scenario can be constructed.

I am not arguing here that all or even most theists understand such coincidences to be miracles. For instance, Piotr Bylica (2015: 317–18) acknowledges that intentional supernatural activity "can produce either effects consistent with the regular natural order or *effects that are surprising and astonishing, which (it can be assumed within a particular system of beliefs) nature itself is not able to produce*" and then adds that "the latter are usually *referred to as miracles*" (emphasis mine). I'm stating only that the category of coincidence miracle is recognized by some theists and, more importantly for our purposes, is frequently discussed by philosophers.

More significantly, though, some appear to believe that we ought not consider divine activity that has a natural explanation available to be miraculous because it blurs the distinction between miracle and divine providence. Martin Luck (2016:275) correctly notes that most theists want to maintain that providence and miracle "are two separate sub-categories of divine action." He then cites Robert Larmer (1988:8), who maintains that providential events are "religiously significant events viewed as indirectly produced by God, events which they feel God designed nature to produce," while miracles are "religiously significant events viewed as directly produced by God (events which would never have occurred had God not overridden the usual course of nature)." If we add to this the fact that Larmer (1988:14) defines a miracle as something "beyond the power of nature to produce," it then follows that we must refrain from considering events with fully natural explanations available to be miraculous if we want to avoid the unwanted result of all or too much divine activity becoming miraculous.

I question Larmer's understanding of divine providence. Most definitions of divine providence focus on the concept of God's sovereign guidance and control of all things, with the accompanying distinction between general providence – God's continuous upholding of the existence and nature of the universe – and special providence – God's intentional intervention in the world to exact some desired end. Defined this way, Larmer's attempt to equate providential events with "events that God designed nature to produce" and miracles with "events that never would have occurred had God not overridden the usual course of nature" in the sense that they are "beyond the power of nature to produce" is, at best, misleading. Rather, a miracle is better understood as just one type of special providence. And if this is so, then the category of coincidence miracles remains a viable concept for consideration.

As we will discuss in later Sections, while this understanding of miracle is subject to what some see as significant epistemological difficulties related to the identification of miracles and to the use of the miraculous to bolster God's existence, this understanding of miracle as an event is least problematic conceptually.

1.2   A Miracle as an Act of God

We will now turn our attention to definitional clarifications related to the ways in which miracles have been understood to be the result of intentional divine activity.

First, while it is true that a miracle, as we are defining it, is an event resulting from intentional supernatural activity, it's important to note that most theists acknowledge that supernatural beings other than God intervene in earthly affairs, even at times to bring about unusual, unexpected occurrences. For example, classical Christian theology contains references to benevolent supernatural beings called angels who engaged in healing activity. Likewise, it is often acknowledged that the intentional activity of malevolent supernatural beings such as Satan and demons are capable of bringing about unusual, even awe-producing, occurrences.

Should our discussion of the miraculous be limited to supernatural intervention by God alone, or should it include intervention by other supernatural beings? Robert Larmer doesn't believe that we should label the interventive activity of malevolent supernatural agents miraculous. However, Larmer (1988:9) also does not believe that benevolent miraculous supernatural intervention should be limited to God:

> Whether or not this agent must be God or whether some lesser created agent might conceivably work a miracle is not always agreed upon. Some philosophers and theologians have wanted to insist that only God can work miracles. Yet, prima facie, it seems conceivable that beings other than God might produce miracles. There seems no absurdity in supposing that an angel might cause a miracle and there are reports in which the alleged agent of the miracle is a person, as in Acts 3: 1–9. To insist that only God can work a miracle is to place upon the term a restriction inconsistent with the way in which it is generally used. Far more plausible is the view that all that is required is an agent who, to some degree, transcends nature.

It is true that many theists believe that supernatural beings other than God *are involved* in miraculous activity. And it is even held by some, as Larmer notes, that some humans – for example, faith healers – have the ability to perform miracles. However, in both cases it is normally assumed that the ultimate source of a miraculous occurrence is God's power, manifesting itself through human or subservient supernatural agents on whom God has bestowed the requisite authority (Randi, 1987; Burgess, McGee, & Alexander, 1988). For this reason, and also because to do so is in keeping with the focus of most philosophical discussions of the miraculous, we will reserve the designation of miracle for events that would not have occurred when and how they did without the intentional direct divine interventive activity of God.

Second, we need to clarify more fully the distinction between direct and indirect divine activity. As we have seen, the majority of theists who acknowledge divine activity in our world believe much of what occurs are acts of God in the broad, fundamental sense that God has created the universe, established the "laws" upon which the natural order is based, and continues to sustain this natural order by divine power. In this sense, a summer thunderstorm or the birth of a baby can be said to be acts of God. At times divine activity of this sort has been, and continues to be, referred to as miraculous. However, as we have seen, most theists also hold that there are some events that would not have occurred in the exact manner in which they did if God had not *directly* intervened in some manner to manipulate the natural order. Miraculous occurrences are normally considered by theists to fall within this category of "direct acts of God."

There isn't uniform agreement, though, on whether God's interventive activity related to coincidence miracles – events that have fully natural explanations available but would not have occurred as they did without divine intervention – should be considered direct acts of God.

Morgan Luck has recently discussed a number of different understandings of the distinction between direct and indirect acts of God and how they relate to what can be considered miracles. For some philosophers, Luck (2016: 268–69) notes, the distinction between direct and indirect (transitive) causation is this:

"An event is a direct cause of another if there are no other events in the causal chain between the two. Inversely, an event is an indirect cause of another if there are additional events in the causal chain between the two." Assuming this distinction, Luck (2016:271) then rightly notes that a miracle defined as a direct act of God is restricted to "a natural effect with a non-natural cause, where there are *no further events* in the causal sequence between the natural effect and non-natural cause" (emphasis mine).

Luck points out that there are those who want to at least allow for additional non-natural events to be introduced into the causal chain. For instance, if God were to command an angel to heal someone, there are those who would want to consider the healing a miracle, even though this scenario involves an additional non-natural event. To accommodate this common perspective, Luck (2016: 272) introduces the concept of a weak direct act of God, in relation to which the definition of a miracle is expanded somewhat to include "a natural effect with a non-natural cause, where there are *no further natural events* in the causal sequence between the natural effect and non-natural cause" (emphasis mine).

Luck acknowledges that some want to go even further, claiming that a natural effect that God brought about by initiating and ensuring a causal chain that included natural events can also be considered a miracle.[1] Luck refers to divine activity of this sort as an indirect act of God. Consider again, for instance, Holland's story of the boy saved from death because of a series of very fortuitous natural events: the engineer of a train faints, causing his hand to release the throttle which, in turn, automatically engages the brake, which causes the train to stop just before hitting a small boy playing on the tracks. Even assuming God caused the sequence of events to occur when and how they did for the purpose of saving the boy, given Luck's terminology, this would be a miracle caused by an indirect act of God.

While others are certainly justified in restricting the scope of a direct act of God in this way, I see no reason why the broader

---

[1] Coincidence miracles are a subset of this category.

understanding with which we have been working is not equally justified. In fact, I believe this broader definition to be more in keeping with what is and has been assumed by those philosophers and theologians discussing the miraculous. Hence, for our purpose we will continue to assume that when an event is (1) the result of the natural order God has established and sustains – for instance, the birth of a baby – and (2) does not involve any intentional divine action that modifies or structures the natural order in such a way to ensure this exact event occurs exactly when and how it did, the event is best considered an indirect act of God. When it is believed that God has intentionally manipulated the natural order to ensure that an event happens exactly when and how it does, it then becomes a direct act of God, regardless of whether a fully natural explanation is available.

Even here a finer distinction is sometimes made with respect to the relationship between coincidence miracles and direct acts of God. When we think of God directly bringing about an event, it is quite reasonable to conceive of God's manipulation of the natural order occurring at the time that the event takes place. In our train scenario, it is quite natural to conceive of God acting in some way just before the train rounds the bend. Or when we think of God healing someone with cancer, it is quite natural to conceive of God intervening at the moment the healing is observable. And most who believe God brought it about that someone misses a fatal flight would be assuming that God did so at the time the person was attempting to reach the airport.

There are philosophers such as Robert Adams, however, who have suggested another way of thinking about God's activity in this context. We can, Adams (1992: 209) tells us, conceive of God creating "the world in such a way that it was physically predetermined from the beginning" that nature would act in the appropriate way "at precisely the time at which God foresaw" it would be needed. We can, for instance, think of God creating the world in such a way that the driver of a specific train on a specific track at a specific time would faint in order to save the life of a young child. Or we can conceive of God creating the world in such a way that the tire on a specific car would be flat at a specific time to ensure that the person driving the car would not arrive at the airport in time to board a fatal flight.

This line of thought can also be found in those rabbis mentioned in the Talmud, who argued that to hold that the walls of Jericho came down at the exact time needed to ensure an Israelite victory was the result of divine intervention does not require believing that God intervened in the natural order at the exact time this event occurred. It can be assumed, rather, that God determined when setting up the natural order that an earthquake would bring down the walls "naturally" at the exact time this event occurred (Midrash Genesis, Midrash Exodus, & Pirkei Avot).

John Polkinghorne (1986:72–73) offers us yet another version of this line of reasoning:

> Some believe that God acts in the world by a combination of fore-sight and ingenious prior fixing. Bringing about such coincidences to produce occasions of significance. It is possible to think about some of the miracles in the Gospels, particularly the nature mira-cles, in this way. We read how Jesus spoke a word and the storm on the lake was stilled. The energy in that Palestinian weather system exceeded that of an atomic bomb. We need not, however, assume that Jesus altered its meteorological structure in a direct act of enormous power. Rather there was a divinely ordained significance in the coming together of the lapsing of the storm through natural process and Jesus saying "Peace. Be still!" The disciples were right indeed to say "Who then is this?" even if we cannot go on with them to say further "even wind and sea obey him", that is how the account would run.

In all these cases, to restate the general point, God is still viewed as directly intervening in the sense that God purposely manipulates the natural order to bring about some event that would not have occurred without this intentional divine activity. However, God is not viewed as directly intervening in the sense that God directly manipulates a natural order already in place. It is held, rather, that the intentional divine activity takes place when God was planning how the natural order would operate and not at the time this predetermined natural activity occurred.[2]

While viewing divine activity in this way is unusual and not in keeping with how most theists or philosophers understand divine intervention, it is not inconsistent with the definition of miracle with which we are working. However, as we will see in Section 4, it is questionable whether this concept of divine intervention is consistent with certain understandings of how God's power relates to human freedom.

1.3 Working Definition of Miracle

What then is a miracle? For the purpose of our discussion, a miracle is being defined as an unusual, unexpected, observable event due in part to the intentional direct interventive activity of God. As we have seen, though, this definition allows for various ways of understanding the nature of the event itself. It is compatible with this definition to assume that the event in question is best understood as a violation or circumvention of the natural order. It's also acceptable to consider as coincidence miracles even events that don't appear incompatible with the natural order.

Likewise, we have seen that this definition allows for various understandings of the ways in which direct divine interventive activity can manifest itself. It is acceptable to view such activity as at times an observable manipulation of the natural order but at other time not. And while it is acceptable to assume that God manipulates the natural order at the time the event occurs, it is also acceptable to assume that the "manipulation" in question is a predetermination on God's part that nature will function in such a way to bring about the desired event at just the right time.

Moreover, as we have seen, there are many other proposed characteristics of the miraculous that are not being included in

---

[2] For theologians such as Calvin and Luther, this distinction in a very real sense collapses since, given this model of divine sovereignty, God has in every case decreed both the event and the means necessary to ensure that it comes about.

the definition we're using for this study. Accordingly, as each definitional understanding of miracle – both those within our working definition and those not – can trigger quite different conceptual, epistemological, and moral issues, it is incumbent on all of us discussing the miraculous to explicitly acknowledge that the conception of miracle with which we are working is but one of many and that the resultant analyses, accordingly, are not necessarily relevant to miracle *simpliciter* but rather primarily to the given conception we have chosen to address.

2 Conceptual Issues

We ended Section 1 with the following working definition of miracle: an unusual, unexpected, observable event due in part to the intentional direct interventive activity of God. This Section is an overview of some key conceptual issues related to the miraculous as both an event and act of God that continue to be discussed by philosophers.

2.1 A Miracle as an Observable Event

With respect to the miraculous as an observable event, there remains significant discussion concerning whether a miracle, if defined as a violation of a natural law, is a coherent concept. The initial argument for the coherence of a violation of a natural law, remember, goes something like this: what we know of well-established natural laws leads us to believe, for instance, that those who have genuinely died do not (at least in a physical sense) come back to life and that water does not turn instantly into wine. Let's assume, though, that someone actually was to rise from the dead or that water did instantly turn into wine. We would be required at that point not only to acknowledge the occurrence of an event that our understanding of natural laws gives us good reason to believe would not occur but, more importantly, we would then be required to acknowledge the occurrence of an event for which it is doubtful there could ever be a fully natural explanation forthcoming. And at that point we would be justified in claiming that a natural law has been violated. However, many find attempts to define a miracle as a violation of natural laws to be fraught with conceptual difficulties.

First, questions arise around the status of natural laws. Most discussions of miracles as "violations" of natural laws presuppose that such laws are deterministic. But as noted in Section 1, if natural laws are indeterministic – for example, "if life depends on chemistry and chemistry depends on atoms and atoms depend on quantum mechanics and quantum mechanics is essentially indeterministic" – it might then seem that God is given more "room" to bring about miracles without reference to the violation of laws (van Inwagen, 2006: 118). It is, of course, true that if the concept of a violation of a natural law is potentially coherent only if such laws are conceived of as deterministic, there can then be no violation if laws are indeterministic. However, the status of natural laws remains a very open question. So we'll continue to assume for our purpose that discussions of violations of nature laws – understood in a deterministic sense – are not irrelevant or confused for this reason (Vicens, 2016: 34).

Second, as Timothy McGrew (2016: section 1.2) notes, it's not always clear which natural law would be violated by an alleged miracle. Take, for instance, the claim that someone has been raised from the dead. We observe that the dead stay dead, but there is no single natural law to this effect. Rather, "the laws involved in the decomposition of a dead body are all at a much more fundamental level, at least at the level of biochemical and thermodynamic processes and perhaps at the level of interactions of fundamental particles." This is a helpful reminder of the complexity of understanding what a violation of any given law would actually entail, but is not itself a conceptual problem.[3]

---

[3] McGrew (2016, section1.2) also maintains that we lose little if we drop consideration of natural laws altogether. "One benefit of defining miracles in terms of violations of natural law is that this definition entails that a miracle is beyond the productive power of nature. But if that is the key idea, then it is hard to see why we should not simply use that as the definition and leave out the problematic talk of laws." While this may be true, philosophical discussions of miracles in terms of natural law continue unabated, so for the purpose of this Element we follow suit.

The most common conceptual concern raised in relation to violation miracles is that to conceive of an event as a violation of natural laws is incoherent. Natural laws, many hold, are simply statements that describe the actual course of events. Accordingly, it could never be the case that we find ourselves justifiably claiming both that our current set of natural laws is adequate and that some acknowledged occurrence is a true violation of (counterinstance to) these laws in the sense that it is an event for which no natural explanation could ever be forthcoming. It may well be that true counterinstances to current laws occur. However, acknowledging that a true counterinstance to established laws has occurred only demonstrates the law(s) in question to be inadequate since we must always be willing, in principle, to expand our natural laws to accommodate any actual occurrence no matter how unusual (McKinnon, 1967).

Or stated more succinctly: "if the natural laws are simply compendious statements of natural regularities, an apparent 'violation' would most naturally be an indication, not that a supernatural intervention in the course of nature had occurred, but rather that what we had thought was a natural law was, in fact, not one" (McGrew, 2016: section 1.2). And if this line of reasoning is correct, then it follows that a violation of our natural laws – viewed as a true counterinstance to true (adequate) laws – is conceptually impossible.

It might appear that we have an easy way out of this problem. As we saw in Section 1, many hold that to claim that natural laws accurately describe the natural order is to say only that such laws correctly predict what will occur under a specified set of natural conditions. However, to maintain that an event is a miraculous counterinstance to a set of natural laws – for instance, that someone has risen from the dead – is not to maintain that some event has occurred under the same set of natural conditions covered by these laws. Rather, it is to claim that an additional non-natural causal factor, namely direct divine activity, was also at play in this case. Or as Mackie (1982: 19–20) states the point: what we consider laws of nature "describe the ways in which the world – including, of

course, human beings – works when left to itself, when not interfered with. A miracle occurs when the world is not left to itself,
when something distinct from the natural order as a whole
intrudes into it." Accordingly, if we assume that those who claim
miracles violate natural laws aren't really saying that the natural
laws in question don't hold, but rather that some non-natural
causal factor was also involved, the seeming conceptual problem
dissolves.

However, this doesn't seem to capture adequately what many
theists have in mind when they claim that miracles can't be given a
fully natural explanation. Many who define miracles as events
contrary to the laws of nature want to use the inability of our
current set of natural laws to accommodate these anomalies as
evidence for divine intervention (and thus God's existence), so they
want to press the point that the events they consider miracles are
true counterinstances to (violations of) true natural laws. And they
mean by this something stronger than simply the fact that if the
event in question is a true miracle – and, thus, is in part the result of
non-natural factors – this event cannot be given a fully natural
explanation.

To help clarify what I think they do mean, I want to introduce a
distinction between *event tokens* and *event types*. It is, of course, the
case that if an event is in part the result of direct divine intervention, this occurrence itself, as an event token, cannot have a totally
natural causal explanation. The primary purpose of natural
science, however, is not to determine what nature has in fact
produced. Rather, the primary objective of science is to determine
what nature is capable of producing under solely natural conditions. With respect to an instance of cancer remission in an individual, for instance, the primary purpose of natural science is not to
decide whether natural factors alone were actually responsible for
any specific person's remission. The primary purpose is to determine whether natural factors alone could have produced this type
of event.

Accordingly, as I see it, those who want to claim that a miracle is
a true counterinstance to a true law are not claiming only that the

anomaly in question, as an event token, is contrary to our present set of laws; they are claiming that the occurrence in question is the type of event that could never be given a fully natural explanation. Hence, the question we need to consider is not whether we could ever be in a position to maintain justifiably that a specific state of affairs, as an event token, was not produced by nature alone. The question, rather, is whether we could ever be in a position to maintain justifiably that an event of this type could not have been produced by natural factors alone (Basinger & Basinger, 1986).[4]

I don't believe that the concept of a permanently inexplicable event type is incoherent or conceptually problematic. I do want to argue, however, that we could never find ourselves in a situation that required the decision in question to be made – that there is no conceivable situation in which we would be required to decide whether a currently inexplicable event type could or could not ever be given a fully natural explanation.

It's clearly the case that science continues to discover new, often startling and unexpected, information about the nature of the causal factors that operate in our universe. The annals of science note many instances in which counterinstances to supposedly well-established natural laws were later demonstrated – sometimes only after significant conceptual shifts in thinking – to in fact be consistent with natural laws or revisions thereof. Would it not, accordingly, be the height of scientific provincialism for anyone to ever decide, solely on the basis of the data presently available, that it was at this time justifiable to label a given event permanently inexplicable by natural causal factors alone? Would it not always be more reasonable for scientists, given our necessarily limited understanding of the natural order, to respond to even the most unusual of incongruities by continuing to run tests indefinitely or by simply labeling the occurrence an anomaly and waiting for the occurrence of similar phenomena before seriously investigating further?

---

[4] This line of reasoning also appears implicitly in Richard Swinburne's writing on miracles (1970: 23–32).

Not all philosophers find this line of reasoning convincing. For example, Richard Swinburne (1970: 32) distinguishes between repeatable and nonrepeatable anomalies and then argues as follows:

> We have to some extent good evidence about what are the "laws of nature", and some of them are so well established and account for so many data that any modification of them which we would suggest to account for the odd counterinstance would be so clumsy and ad hoc that it would upset the whole structure of science. For example, let us imagine we experience the "resurrection from the dead ... a man whose heart has not been beating for twenty-four hours and who was dead by other currently used criteria" or "water turning into wine without the assistance of chemical apparatus or catalysts." It would be most reasonable in such cases for the scientist to label such phenomena ... permanently inexplicable events.

Or as McGrew (2016: section 1:2) correctly (I believe) interprets Swinburne on this point:

> If a putative law has broad scope, great explanatory power, and appealing simplicity, it may be more reasonable ... to retain the law (defined as a regularity that virtually invariably holds) and to accept that the event in question is a non-repeatable counter-instance of that law than to throw out the law and create a vastly more complex law that accommodates the event.

Margaret Boden (1969) offers a similar line of reasoning. While she grants that observable phenomena cannot normally be dismissed as lying forever outside the range of science, she is not convinced this would always be the case. Let us consider, she asks, the logically possible case of a leper whose missing fingers reappear instantly under very stringent, fraud-detecting conditions, such as in the presence of doctors or TV cameras. This occurrence, she argues, would conflict with so many accepted scientific facts that any attempt on our part to revise our present scientific laws to accommodate an event of this type would so weaken the predictive power of such laws that they would no longer be of practical value.

Accordingly, she concludes, if such an event were actually to occur, scientists would be forced to acknowledge it to be a permanently unexplainable phenomenon.

While this line of reason might have some prima facie appeal, it seems to me my question still holds. Both Swinburne and Boden freely acknowledge that science continues to discover new, unanticipated information about the causal factors and relationships that govern our universe. They also acknowledge freely that our scientific records note numerous examples of when supposed counterinstances to longstanding scientific laws were later demonstrated to be consistent with such laws or revisions of them. Accordingly, how can they believe that anyone can justifiably maintain solely on the basis of the data now available to us that certain event types could justifiably be labeled permanently unexplainable?

It's important to note that the reason Swinburne and Boden believe we can – at least in principle – justifiably label an occurrence permanently inexplicable is not, as mentioned before, because they believe they have some privileged understanding of the true nature of reality. Rather, it is because they believe that if faced with an event acknowledged by all to be a true counterinstance to very highly confirmed laws, there are only two options: to either modify the laws to accommodate the event or affirm the adequacy of the laws and declare the event permanently unexplainable. And in some conceivable cases, they conclude, the latter would be the more reasonable choice.

As I see it, however, we are here being presented with a false dilemma. I deny that given certain real or imaginable occurrences that appear to be counterinstances to well-established laws, we must either declare the type of event in question permanently inexplicable naturally or declare that there is a fully natural explanation (even if it is yet to be found). The most reasonable response, I still contend, remains the third option noted earlier: to acknowledge that the type of event in question might be inexplicable naturally but to continue to search for a natural explanation. I do not see that to do so would functionally damage the natural laws in question since, as Swinburne acknowledges, it is only repeatable or frequent counterinstances that falsify natural laws. Or to state this important point differently: unless the type of event in question were repeatable naturally or occurred over and over, the practical value of the relevant natural laws in question for predicting activity in the natural order would remain.

Holland (1965: 43) seems to believe that this third option would place the relevant laws in a state of uncertainty and would therefore weaken the strength of the scientific method. I don't deny that counterinstances to our current natural laws challenge the reliability of such laws. In fact, as I've just stated, *if* the occurrence of acknowledged counterinstances to well-established laws required that we either modify such laws immediately or declare the counterinstances to be permanently unexplainable, the latter might well in some cases be the most reasonable choice. However, again, only *repeatable* counterinstances actually require us to make such a decision. In relation to *nonrepeatable* counterinstances – no matter how unusual and surprising – the third alternative noted is always open to us: to continue to assume the functional adequacy of the current laws in question while searching for new or modified laws to accommodate the anomaly in question.

More recently, Frank Jankunis (2014: 595) has acknowledged that when faced with a nonrepeatable counterinstance to a law of nature, one option (my third option) is to "shelve the anomaly as unexplained pending the results of future investigation and the resulting improved understanding of their world." And he acknowledges that "this option is a measure of humility, a recognition that the end of science has not yet come ... coupled with a hope that the progress necessary to understand what has happened will occur soon. Perhaps it will even be necessary, once more is learned, to revise the laws of the sphere."

However, Jankunis is not totally convinced this is the manner in which every anomalous event should be handled. The greater the amount of objective evidence for the validity (accuracy) of the laws with which an unusual event is currently inconsistent, Jankunis (2014: 596–97) maintains, the better case we have for claiming the event "has a supernatural causal explanation and is, thus, permanently inexplicable naturally." Not to allow that we could come to the place that we rightly decided an event is best labeled permanently inexplicable is to assume illegitimately that there is no supernatural agent capable of directly intervening to bring about the event in question.

The position Jankunis is supporting seems to me based on a confusion related to our distinction between an event token and an event type. To claim, as I do, that it is always best to continue to acknowledge the functional adequacy of the current laws in question while we search for new or modified laws to accommodate an unusual occurrence does not commit one in any way to saying that there are no supernatural agents or that supernatural agents don't causally intervene in earthly affairs in ways that result in event tokens that do not have fully natural explanations. As I've repeatedly acknowledged, if we were to come to the point where we believe justifiably that an event token was the result of direct divine intervention, this event could obviously never be given a fully natural explanation – it would be permanently unexplainable naturally.

To state this important point differently, the position I'm holding is, contra Jankunis, non-problematic for the theist who affirms the occurrence of miracles. Given our distinction between event type and event token, for a theist to agree that we should always continue to assume the functional adequacy of the current laws in question and welcome scientific efforts to discover new or modified laws to accommodate the unusual occurrence in question, doesn't in any sense entail that certain event tokens can't be held justifiably by these theists to be occurrences for which no fully natural explanation could be forthcoming and, thus, considered candidates for the miraculous.

So my contention, I believe, still stands. If our natural laws at present are unable to accommodate events of this type, there is no scientific need to claim that the event type will never be explicable naturally. Furthermore, leaving open the question of whether any event type is permanently inexplicable has the added benefit of removing the awkward, functionally unnecessary need for scientists (or any of us) to make predictions concerning the future limits of scientific explanation.

That this is so could well be one of the reasons why the definition of a miracle as an occurrence whose event type could never be given a natural explanation is sometimes replaced with a definition in which it is claimed only that a miracle is an unusual, unexpected, observable divinely induced occurrence that has *at present* no fully natural explanation as an event type. In the *American Heritage Dictionary* (2000) we read, for instance, that a miracle is "an event that *appears inexplicable* by the laws of nature" (emphasis added).

I grant, though, that my position does have an important epistemological implication. If we should always leave the natural explicability status of event type an open question, then we will never be in a position to claim that a miracle, defined as the type of event for which a natural explanation could never be given, has actually occurred. At the very least, any decision to label an event a miracle because it seems to us so highly unlikely that a fully natural explanation for an event of this type could be forthcoming would have to be made tentatively, since it is always possible that science will in the future be able to furnish a fully natural explanation for the type of event in question. Or, as Theodore Drange (1998) rightly states this point: "If events which cannot at present be explained ... were to come to be explained naturalistically in the future, then, in retrospect, it would need to be said of them that they were never miracles, although they may at one time have (erroneously) been thought to be that." In turn, if this is so, then the apologetical force of any unexplainable event – the ability of any unexplainable event to enhance the probability of the existence of a supernatural agent capable of bringing about such an event – is at least to some extent weakened.

Before moving to the consideration of conceptual issues related to the claim that a miracle is at least in part the result of intentional divine activity, I want to note that we are now also in a better position to clarify the role of natural law in coincidence miracles

– those significant, unexpected events that involve direct divine intervention although a fully natural explanation is available. To claim that an event – for example, having a flat tire on the way to the airport and, for this reason, missing a plane that crashed – is a coincidence miracle is to acknowledge that the event type in question has a fully natural explanation – that is, that the natural order can on its own bring about events of this type. However, it is also to claim that nature itself did not in fact produce fully the event token in question. It is to agree with Levine (2005: introduction) that a miracle can never be "a mere coincidence no matter how extraordinary or significant. (If you miss a plane and the plane crashes, that is not a miracle unless God intervened in the natural course of events causing you to miss the flight)." As an event token, an observed occurrence cannot be considered a miracle, "no matter how remarkable, unless the 'coincidence' itself is caused by divine intervention (i.e., [is] not really a coincidence at all)."

2.2 A Miracle as an Act of God

We'll turn now to issues related to the coherence of the concept of direct divine intervention in earthly affairs.

One prominent voice on miracle, David Corner, argues that any conception of the miraculous that is built upon supernatural *causation* – that is, an understanding of the miraculous that assumes that God is the main causal force in the occurrence of the event in question and, therefore, that the event itself could not have been produced by nature alone – is problematic. Specifically, the concept of a supernatural causal force overriding or modifying the relevant natural causes, he points out, is very difficult to explicate coherently (Corner, 2007). Moreover, it is possible, Corner (2007: 3) notes, to speak meaningfully about an agent performing a basic action – for instance, a person moving a body part – "without being committed to a *causal* analysis of what she has done." Accordingly, he concludes, it is best not to understand a miracle as an instance of supernatural causality superseding or modifying these laws. The best understanding of miracle, rather, is one that views the miraculous as a basic divine action that "contradicts any reasonable expectations about what is going to happen" but is in need of no causal explanation vis-à-vis the natural order (2007: 14–16).

I agree that any attempt to offer an adequate causal analysis (of the type Corner has in mind) for how a supernatural entity can override, suspend, or modify the natural order would be difficult or not even possible. It doesn't seem to me, though, that this is an insurmountable critique of the type of causal account of the miraculous in question – a causal account that holds that the occurrences in question are the result in part of supernatural activity – since to view miracle in this way does not commit one to being able to explicate such causation or even understand exactly how such causation is possible in the sense Corner has in mind. Rather, it is to make what I see as the coherent and justifiable causal claim that the event in question would not have come about when and how it did if God had not intentionally decided that it should and did not do what is necessary (whatever that might be) to ensure its occurrence.

A different type of challenge to direct divine intervention, as already noted, centers on the rationality of believing in the existence of a being capable of intervening in earthly affairs. One form of this challenge comes from those who maintain that it is irrational (not justifiable) for anyone to believe that God (as a supernatural agent who can intentionally intervene) exists. For instance, Richard Dawkins, in his popular and influential book *The God Delusion* (2006), speaks for a number of past and present thinkers when he contends not only that it is highly improbable that God exists but that religious faith qualifies as a delusional false belief. However, while I grant that these nontheists are justified in believing personally that no supernatural being capable of intervention in the natural order exists, no such critic has, in my estimation – and in that of many philosophers of religion – established in an objective, non-question-begging manner that theists cannot justifiably believe both that a supernatural being exists and that such a being intentionally acts in our world (Plantinga, 2000; Basinger, 2002: 31–53).

What is less frequently acknowledged, or at least discussed in this context, is that there exists a prominent group of theists, namely Process Theists, who also deny the existence of a God who can intervene unilaterally in earthly affairs.[5] As theists, they don't, of course, deny the existence of God. However, Process Theists do maintain that God cannot unilaterally control any state of affairs. All entities always retain some power of self-determination. God is always trying to persuade (lure) us to make the best choices but can never unilaterally intervene in human or natural activity. And this means, of course, to be even more specific, that God cannot intervene unilaterally in earthly affairs to override, circumvent, or in any other sense directly manipulate the natural order to bring about miraculous events (Cobb & Griffin, 1976).

However, while many Process Theists believe that their conceptual understanding of God is alone coherent and rational, I agree with those who believe this contention to be too strong. While I grant that the Process understanding of God is conceptually coherent, I agree with those who contend that Process Theists have not successfully demonstrated on the basis of objective, non–question-begging criteria that the conception of God required for miraculous intervention is incoherent or irrational. And, again, this is sufficient for our purposes (Basinger, 1988).

The final conceptual clarification related to divine intervention to be considered centers on the coherence of maintaining, as many theists do, that humans can influence God's decision to intervene in miraculous ways through petitionary prayer. The relationship between miracle and petitionary prayer will be discussed in detail in Section 4. However, I want to point out now a conceptual difficulty inherent in one prominent understanding of the relationship between divine control and human freedom. Proponents of what is often labeled Theological Determinism maintain that God *is* all-controlling. Humans are free and responsible for their actions, but all and only that which God has determined (decreed) should

---

[5] For Process Theists, this is not a divine choice; it is a metaphysical reality.

happen does happen. In short, whatever it means for humans to be free, God controls all that humans "freely" say and do (Basinger, 2013).

Let's assume at this point that this compatibilistic understanding of human freedom is coherent and focus on the following question: Does God sometimes directly intervene in response to a request to bring about a "miraculous" event that (1) God desired to occur and was able to ensure would occur but that (2) would not have occurred – God would not have intervened to bring about – if the request had not been made?

For the Theological Determinist, the answer is clearly no. The Theological Determinist can rightly claim that human petitioning is a causal component in the overall plan ordained by God to bring about desired divine ends. However, since the God of Theological Determinism can control "free" human choice, it can never be the case that a human decision outside of God's control is a necessary determining factor in whether God will act miraculously in our world. Or, to state this important point differently: within Theological Determinism – which remains a very common and widespread understanding of God's divine control over earthly affairs – the status of human freedom vis-à-vis divine control presupposed does not allow free human decision-making to be posited coherently as a necessary causal component that determines whether a miracle will actually occur.[6]

3 Epistemic Issues

We are defining the miraculous as an unusual, unexpected, observable event due in part to the intentional direct interventive activity of God. Section 2 was an overview of some key conceptual issues related to the miraculous as both an event and an act of God. In this

---

[6] We'll see in Section 4 that there is another common understanding of divine control in relation to which it is conceptually possible (although morally challenging) for God to intervene miraculously in response to human petitioning.

Section we will discuss some key epistemic issues related to these two components of a miracle.

3.1   A Miracle as an Unusual Event

In Section 2, we concluded that the standard characterizations of a miraculous event vis-à-vis the natural order – as a violation, circumvention, or coincidence – are all coherent concepts. Is it rational, though, to believe that such events have occurred or even could actually occur? Since coincidence miracles are not as event types incompatible with our current laws of nature (what is unusual and unexpected is the timing and impact of the event in question), such events – qua events – raise no significant epistemic concerns. That is, if events have natural explanations available, as is the case in Holland's story about the boy and the train (Section 1), the accuracy of such claims can be assessed in the same way we assess any historical report. We can, for example, try to determine whether the original source was trustworthy and whether what was originally reported has been faithfully transmitted.

Such is not the case, however, with respect to circumvention and violation miracles, where in both cases what's being claimed is that the event in question has, at least at present, no fully natural explanation given our current understanding of the natural order. While we will later discuss the adequacy of the evidence for one specific event – the resurrection of Jesus – we will now discuss the general question of whether there are conditions under which it would be justifiable to maintain that an event that is allegedly unexplainable naturally has occurred as reported. Are there conditions, for example, under which a person could justifiably maintain that water had turned into wine or someone's leg has been lengthened instantly? It's important to emphasize that this question is separable from the question of whether it is rational to maintain that God intentionally brought about some event. The two questions can be related. In fact, as we have seen, some base the rationality of the belief that an event is naturally inexplicable on the rationality of belief that the event was caused by God, and vice versa. But there is no necessary connection between the claim that an event occurred as reported and the claim that it was brought about by God.

As was noted in Section 2, most philosophers currently grant that reports of repeatable counterinstances to current natural laws cannot justifiably be dismissed – that is, they grant that if counterinstances to our current laws recur, given equivalent natural conditions, revision of the relevant laws must be considered. However, the types of counterinstances often considered to be miraculous by theists – for example, resurrections and healings – are at present not repeatable under specifiable natural conditions. There are a number of philosophers who maintain that when assessing the accuracy of reports of events of this type, much greater skepticism is required. The updated version of David Hume's cautionary argument offered by Antony Flew (1976) succinctly captures why some still believe such skepticism is warranted.

Flew acknowledges the possibility that nonrepeatable counterinstances to well-confirmed natural laws have occurred (or will occur). However, he continues, Hume has rightly pointed out that the wise person proportions his or her belief to the evidence. And when the evidence is considered rationally, the problem at hand becomes apparent. There are highly confirmed natural laws on the basis of which we justifiably believe, for example, that water does not turn into wine, withered legs do not return to normal instantaneously, and the dead remain dead. These laws are not based on inaccessible scientific studies or outmoded historical hearsay. Rather, these laws can be tested by anyone at any time, with the result always the same: untreated water persists as water; withered legs remain malformed; and the dead stay dead.

Such is not the case with reports of alleged miraculous events. Reported counterinstances to natural laws are supported only by personal testimony from the past, with evidence of this sort by its very nature always weaker than the evidence for the laws it allegedly contradicts. One reason the evidence is always weaker is that while large numbers of people testing independently continue to find the laws in question to hold, only a small number of possibly biased individuals maintain that the counterinstance occurred. Moreover, the evidence supporting the laws in question is objective, while the testimonial reports of those who claim to have witnessed the event are always quite subjective.

Accordingly, Flew continues, there can never be stronger reasons for accepting the report of a nonrepeatable counterinstance to our current laws – for example, the claim that water turned into wine – than for rejecting the report as inaccurate. Again, if an occurrence of the unusual event were repeatable in the sense that it could be reproduced by anyone under specifiable natural conditions, we would then need to take it seriously. However, with respect to reports of nonrepeatable counterinstances, Flew (1976:28–30) concludes, "no matter how impressive the testimony might appear, the most favorable verdict history could ever return must be the agnostic and appropriately Scottish 'not proven'."[7]

Or as Alan Hájek (2008: 88) has more recently stated this Humean conclusion, the "proof" supporting testimonial reports of nonrepeatable counterinstances can never be more compelling than the "proof" from experience against the actual occurrence of the event in question, so "testimony to a miraculous event should never be believed – belief in a miracle report could never be justified."[8]

Can it not be justifiably claimed, though, that this line of reasoning demonstrates an arbitrary and dogmatic naturalistic prejudice? By what right do Flew and others assume that the laws of nature have the ultimate or final voice in relation to history? Can other, non-natural factors be ruled out automatically? For instance, the reason many theists believe that specific miraculous events have occurred is because they are found in sacred texts such as the Bible, the accuracy of which is believed to be guaranteed by their divine origin. Furthermore, as we will discuss in detail later, the types of

[7] J. L. Mackie (1982: 18–29) is one of a number of nontheists who are sympathetic to the Hume/Flew line of reasoning but want to argue only that such considerations make the occurrence of an allegedly miraculous event *"prima facie* unlikely on any particular occasion."

[8] It should be noted that Hájek (2008: 88) then goes on to critique this claim.

miracles recorded in such revelations are often thought to furnish theists with helpful information about the ways God still works in the world today. In short, many theists do in fact believe non-natural evidence to be quite relevant in this context. How then can Flew simply dismiss such evidence completely?

This criticism is misguided. Flew (1967) emphasizes repeatedly that he is, in this context, only discussing what can be concluded on the basis of the historical (natural) evidence alone. He is not attempting to rule out the possibility that the historicity of certain events could, for some people, be settled on the basis of non-natural criteria such as a revelation from God. Furthermore, I don't believe that Flew's decision to consider only "natural" historical criteria is in this context unjustifiable. He considers only evidence of this sort because he is assuming that theists quite often want to use miracles to help establish or support religious belief, and he correctly recognizes that an alleged miracle can have this desired apologetic value only if, among other things, the occurrence in question can be established objectively on natural grounds.

Or, to state this point differently, Flew restricts his discussion to natural historical data because he rightly notes that theists desiring to use the actual occurrence of certain historical events to support religious beliefs – e.g., that God exists and has shared with us authoritative information about what has occurred – cannot base their claim that certain events have actually occurred as reported in part on the assumption that the very religious beliefs whose truth these theists want to establish or bolster are already clearly true.

There are, of course, a number of theists who do not desire or even believe it is possible to verify to the satisfaction of all rational people that particular allegedly miraculous events have actually occurred as reported. They are only interested in establishing that they are justified in believing this for themselves. It is also true, however, that a number of theists have historically and currently wanted to use miracles to support belief in God's existence or support the claim that a given text is an authentic divine revelation

(Corner, 2017: section 2). Accordingly, to the extent that this is still the case, Flew's line of reasoning can't, I believe, be accused of involving arbitrary, dogmatic naturalistic assumptions. In this context, the question of how the actual occurrence of reported events can be authenticated in a public, objective sense remains paramount.

Even granting all this, is Flew's line of reasoning sound? No one questions that natural laws are continuously open to confirmation or disconfirmation and, therefore, that such laws can justifiably be used to predict in general what will or will not occur under certain conditions. For instance, no one denies that we have well-established laws that lead us to believe justifiably that humans do not come to life after three days and, therefore, that we should not expect such an occurrence. Furthermore, few maintain that reports of nonrepeatable counterinstances to well-established current natural laws should not be viewed with a healthy dose of initial skepticism. However, I am among those who believe that we are not justified in assuming that the evidence supporting even the most highly confirmed laws would always furnish a sufficient basis for dismissing reports of nonrepeatable counterinstances to them.

First, it has been noted by some (rightly, I believe) that if what is really being claimed here is that the evidence for the verity of the report of a nonrepeatable counterinstance to a highly confirmed law can never be sufficient to outweigh the evidence supporting the contention that the law has no counterinstance, then we greatly hinder the exploratory work of science (Corner, 2017: section 5).

Second, to make this assumption fails to consider the prima facie reliability of our sensory belief-forming faculties, as championed most recently by proponents of Reformed Epistemology (Scott, 2018.: section 2). In general, it is argued, these faculties serve us quite well. In fact, the general reliability of such faculties must be presupposed by those formulating our natural laws. Accordingly, in those situations where there is no reason to doubt of the reliability of these belief-forming faculties – for instance, if a seeming counterinstance were directly observed by a friend whose character and objectivity were beyond question or if we observed it ourselves – it is not clear that it would always be justifiable to decide in favor of the natural laws in question, even if such laws were very well established and the occurrence in question could not be repeated.

Furthermore, adds Richard Swinburne (1970), it's not the case that we have only the assumed reliability of our belief-forming faculties and the evidence supporting the relevant natural laws to consider. We might also have available some relevant physical traces. For instance, in the case of an alleged lengthening of a deformed leg, we might have X-rays (or photographs) of the leg taken just before and just after the alleged occurrence. An even more compelling physical trace would be a videotape of the incident. It is, of course, true that all of these traces could be altered, so no such physical trace could conclusively verify that the event had actually occurred as reported. Moreover, caution in drawing a conclusion would indeed be justified since the traces would in this case be incompatible with well-established natural laws. However, we have at our disposal generally accepted methods for assessing the authenticity of X-rays, photographs, and videotapes, and if such assessment made it highly likely that such traces were reliable, Swinburne contends, such data would justifiably stand as very strong evidence for the accuracy of the report in question.

Robert Larmer (1988: 95) agrees. When considering the report of an unusual or unexpected event, "the principled interpretation of three kinds of evidence: personal observation; relevant physical traces; and the testimony of others" could make belief that the event has actually occurred quite plausible.

In short, it appears to some, myself included, that there is no justifiable a priori basis for refusing automatically to acknowledge the accuracy of reports of nonrepeatable counterinstances to our current natural laws. The fact that any alleged event is incompatible with well-established natural laws does count strongly against the veracity of the report of its occurrence. Moreover, it might not be easy in any given case to determine exactly when the assumed reliability of our faculties and/or the physical evidence could justifiably be held to counterbalance or even outweigh the long-standing scientific evidence on which the relevant laws are based. However, a decision concerning the accuracy of such reports, I agree, must finally be made on a case-by-case basis.

3.2 A Miracle as an Act of God

In Section 2, we also concluded that the concept of intentional, direct, interventive divine activity is coherent. However, under what conditions, if any, could a person justifiably claim that God has in fact directly intervened in earthly affairs?

Identifying such conditions is most problematic, of course, in relation to coincidence miracles since, by definition, there are for such occurrences fully natural explanations available. In fact, if the question is whether there are conditions under which all rational individuals would be required to acknowledge that an event that has a fully natural explanation available was actually brought about by God's tinkering with the natural order, the answer is clearly no. However, can a theist justifiably maintain that God did in fact manipulate the natural order to bring about some state of affairs – for instance, bring it about that someone had a flat tire so that person would miss a fatal flight?

Christine Overall (2014: 602) thinks not. The problem with a coincidence miracle, she tells us, is that

> an event that is merely unexpected and impressive but nonetheless consistent with empirical laws is potentially fully explicable naturalistically. Its impressiveness and unexpectedness would be simply a function of human beings' lack of knowledge. It would be not just inappropriate and unnecessary but positively contrary to the norms of good investigation to postulate a perfect God as its cause.

Overall is clearly correct in arguing that coincidence miracles do (not just potentially but actually) have fully natural explanations available. Furthermore, I've already acknowledged that this reduces the apologetical value of such events – that is, reduces the likelihood that a nontheist who acknowledges that the event in question occurred as reported will for that reason find the contention that there exists a God who intervenes in earthly affairs more plausible or even less unreasonable.

However, I don't accept that it follows from this that it is positively contrary to the norms of good investigation for a theist to justifiably maintain that God was actually in part the cause of a coincidence occurrence. As I've noted previously, I do not believe that anyone has produced objective non–question-begging criteria in relation to which it can be demonstrated that a God capable of manipulating the natural order does not exist. Moreover, as I will argue in detail later, I believe that theists who affirm any of the three conceptualizations of miraculous events – as coincidences, violations, or circumventions – can reasonably appeal to divine action patterns to justifiably contend that a given event was brought about in part by direct divine intervention. So as I see it, a theist need not acknowledge that the impressiveness and unexpectedness of an alleged coincidence miracle is simply a function of the theist's lack of knowledge and that, accordingly, for a theist to maintain that God was directly involved is unjustifiable or even inappropriate.

Turning now to miracles understood as circumventions or violations of the natural order, one of the key epistemological questions is whether there are conceivable conditions under which all rational individuals would be forced to admit that God has directly intervened to bring about a given occurrence.

Grace Jantzen (1979: 325) is among those who believe that an affirmative answer is required. Let us assume, she begins, that we have compelling evidence for believing that Jesus rose from the dead. If this were in fact the case, any attempt to revise the relevant natural law could hardly be the appropriate response, since what could be gained by revising this law to read, "All men are mortal except those who have an unknown quality, observed on only one occasion and hitherto accountable for only by divine intervention"? In a case such as this where we have "a single exception to a perfectly well-established and well-understood law, and one that is inexplicable unless one appeals to divine intervention ... the skeptical response would be inadequate."

Robert Larmer (1984: 4–10) offers us a similar argument. We are asked to assume not only that we hear of a "man who claims to perform miracles of healing through the power of God" but that we are "able to capture on film occasions when, immediately following the prayers of this man, fingers lost to leprosy were regrown to their original form and length in a matter of seconds, and occasions when eyes severely burned by acid were immediately restored to sight." And let us also assume, we are asked, "not only that this man appears to have the power to heal any kind of disease or injury, but also that no interposition of any [object or force] has any effect on his apparent ability to heal" and that "his power is apparently independent of distance, since people in distant countries have experienced dramatic healing after this man prayed for their cure." The most rational response in such a case, Larmer concludes, would clearly be to acknowledge God's interventive activity. Not to do so is uncritical, dogmatic, and question-begging. Or as Larmer (1988: 114) states the general point in another context: "if an event can be satisfactorily explained by theism as being a miracle, but physicalism can offer no satisfactory explanation of it, then we are justified in seeing it as independent evidence for the superiority of theism over physicalism."

It must be noted here that neither Jantzen nor Larmer is arguing simply that direct divine intervention can justifiably be considered a plausible causal explanation when it cannot be shown that nature, left to her own devices, could produce a given event. Their claim is stronger: if some conceivable events were to occur, it would be most reasonable for all rational individuals to assume that God has directly intervened.

Some have claimed this to be a circular argument. Overall (2003a: 126) maintains, for instance, that the "definition of 'miracle' [in question], which incorporates the idea of supernatural causation, incorporates the very point at issue: that a supernatural being causes miracles ... [so this] definition of 'miracle' short-circuits the whole debate by begging the question."

However, as Frank Jankunis (2014: 592–94) rightly points out, Larmer (and thus by extension, Jantzen) clearly understands that to establish that a miracle has occurred is a two-step process. What must be established is both that the event in question has occurred as reported and that this event is the result of divine intervention. What Larmer is arguing is that if we have established the event in question has occurred as reported, and then that the explanatory hypothesis that God has caused this event is clearly superior to any fully natural explanatory hypothesis, we can justifiably maintain that the event was the result of divine intervention and thus a miracle. And there appears to be nothing circular in this line of reasoning.

There is, though, another concern Jankunis (2014) points out that we must consider more seriously. Does the fact that Larmer (and by extension Jantzen) is a self-avowed theist somehow taint his argument that there are conditions under which it would be most plausible to conclude that divine intervention is the best explanation? Overall believes so. She argues that Larmer's argument is methodologically circular in the sense that the conclusion that there are conditions under which it would be most plausible to assume divine intervention only follows if it is already assumed that the divine being in question exists and is capable of intervening in the relevant sense.

Again, I don't see the alleged circularity. Larmer does in fact happen to believe that a divine being capable of intervening in earthly affairs exists. But this belief has no formal standing in his argument, which is that if a person were to accept that certain events actually occurred, then that person, whether beforehand a theist, atheist, or agnostic, would have to agree that a divine being with the interventive powers in question exists. However, unless it can be established on the basis of objective criteria accepted by all that it's not justifiable to assume the existence of such a being – and I've already stated that I don't think any objective argument to this end has been produced to date – then I don't see how it can be said that Larmer's acknowledged theism makes his claim circular or question-begging.

However, there is a sense – although not her intended sense – in which I believe Overall's focus on Larmer's assumption that there exists a divine being capable of intervening in earthly affairs raises a relevant challenge to Larmer's claim that there are conditions under which it would be most rational for all to acknowledge divine interventive activity. We cannot assess the plausibility of assuming that a divine being exists and is the cause of a given occurrence by considering only evidence for the existence of this being gleaned from the scenario in which this occurrence is embedded. We must consider the plausibility of this being's existence, given all we experience – that is, given all relevant scenarios involving this being. For us to assume, for instance, that remarkable healings of the type noted by Larmer and Jantzen are the result of direct divine intervention is to assume not only that God exists – given the scenarios they mention – but also that this assumption is reasonable given all the experiential scenarios relevant to divine existence and interventive activity. It is to assume, for example, that God's existence is compatible with the amount and types of evil we experience. And this means that if a healing of the type Larmer and Jantzen would have us envision were to occur, the crucial question would not be, as Jantzen and Larmer imply, whether divine causation is the most plausible causal explanation for this occurrence alone. The crucial question would be whether direct divine intervention is the most plausible explanation, given all occurrences in which God can be said to play an active or passive causal role (Basinger, 1987).

McGrew (2016: section 4.2) agrees. In the final analysis, he tells us:

> The relevance of background beliefs looms large ... one's considered rational judgment regarding the existence and nature of God must take into account far more than the evidence for miracle claims ... neither a positive nor a negative claim regarding the existence of God can be established on the basis of evidence for a miracle claim alone, without any consideration of other aspects of the question.

Let us assume that, when comparing the plausibility of believing both that God has healed an individual and has created a world with the amount and types of evil we experience, with the plausibility of believing that God's existence is not compatible with the evil we experience and, thus, that the healing in question must have a natural explanation, someone decides that the latter is more plausible. Would it be justifiable for Jantzen or Larmer to accuse this person of being stubborn or intellectually dishonest? Larmer (1994) seems to believe so. Specifically, he maintains that there are conceivable contexts (such as the one he is having us consider) in which every rational person would have to acknowledge that the evidence for God's existence is so strong that it clearly outweighs any evidence against God's existence – for instance, that generated by evil.

I disagree. Larmer's contention is based on the assumption that we possess (or could in principle possess) a set of neutral, objective, non–question-begging criteria for belief assessment in relation to which we can objectively determine the comparative strength of the evidence for and against God's existence. However, while I do believe that we can objectively determine whether arguments for and against God's existence are self-consistent and comprehensive, I do not believe there exists any set of objective, non–question-begging criteria for comparatively assessing the competing self-consistent, comprehensive perspectives in question. Rather, the comparative assessment of evidence for and against God's existence will, by its very nature, ultimately always be in part a subjective, relative matter (Basinger, 2002; Plantinga, 1979).

What, though, if we modify the question? Rather than asking whether there are imaginable conditions under which all rational individuals would have to acknowledge direct divine intervention, what if the question becomes whether the theist can (could) justifiably claim that divine activity has played a necessary causal role in the occurrence of certain events; that is, whether there are conditions under which the theist can reasonably claim that certain events are direct acts of God?

If we approach this question from purely a defensive posture, the answer, I believe, is yes. If there is no set of neutral, non-question-begging criteria for belief assessment in relation to which we can objectively determine the comparative strength of the evidence for and against God's existence, then the theist will be justified in believing that God was the cause of the event in question in the absence of stronger objective evidence for a fully natural explanation.

However, there are many theists who do not want to speak of justification in this context merely in defensive terms. They possess what they see as positive reasons for maintaining that God does (or at least can) directly intervene in earthly affairs. Specifically, as noted earlier, many theists believe that much of what we know about God and how God might act in our world is gleaned from revelation of a written, oral, or personal type. As Corner sees it (Corner, 2017 section 2), such "revelatory sources for our knowledge of God might, for example, include some form of *a priori* knowledge, super sensory religious experience, or a direct communication by God of information that would not otherwise be available to us." Furthermore, many theists claim that they have acquired from such revelation accurate information about God's general "patterns of action" in our world and that, therefore, when they observe (or at least if they were to observe) some specific occurrence fitting into such a pattern, they can (or at least could) justifiably label it a direct, interventive act of God.[9]

It is important to emphasize that those affirming this divine action pattern thesis are not arguing that God can act only in ways consistent with recognized patterns. They acknowledge that God may well – in fact, quite likely does – intervene in world affairs in ways we cannot understand. The claim is only that divine action patterns do help us understand some of the ways God does

---

[9] It should be noted that many theists also believe they are justified in affirming certain malevolent supernatural action patterns – for instance, that the devil causes suffering to innocent people – and thus believe they are at times justified in attributing a given instance of innocent suffering to malevolent supernatural activity.

intervene. Moreover, in no such case are theists professing absolute certainty. They are claiming only that they are justified in believing that it is more likely than not that a given occurrence is a direct act of God if it is an instantiation of a recognized divine action pattern.

Of course, even given these clarifications, an important question remains. Are the theists in question justified in assuming that the sources from which the divine action patterns are derived – written revelation, tradition, or personal religious experience – yield accurate, trustworthy information? Perhaps in some specific cases such an assumption is not reasonable. For instance, perhaps it can be shown that specific patterns affirmed by some Christians cannot actually be supported by proper biblical interpretation or by correct knowledge of Christian tradition.

However, since I am in that camp of philosophers who maintain that God's existence cannot be conclusively disproved or that the concept of divine communication with humans can be demonstrated to be self-contradictory on the basis of objective, non-question-begging criteria, it should not be surprising that I hold that theists can rationally believe in the accuracy of certain divine action patterns and thus can justifiably label events that fit such patterns direct acts of God.

It's important to acknowledge at this point, however, that whether a given theist believes that a specific divine action pattern actually applies and was actually instantiated in relation to a given event will almost always remain a function, in part, of this theist's prior understanding of how God works in our world – of the set of divine action patterns already affirmed. The differing ways in which Christians respond to faith healers is a good example of the significance such background beliefs can have. Those theists who believe that God currently works through men and women of faith to bring about healing that would not have occurred without intentional divine manipulation of the natural order quite readily allow that reported healings of this sort can, in principle, be considered miraculous divine interventions.

However, some Christians do not believe that the "gifts of the spirit," including the miraculous gift of healing, are still available to believers today. They do not deny that God has in the past healed through individuals or that God can and does today miraculously heal individuals directly. Rather, these Christians believe that, while the gift of healing (along with the other gifts) was in early church history a way of validating the divinely sanctioned religious teachings of certain individuals – a way of demonstrating that such individuals were divinely anointed transmitters of religious truth – such validation became unnecessary once God's primary means of doctrinal revelation, the Bible, was completed and available. Accordingly, for these Christians the alleged healings performed by individuals today are not considered miraculous, even if we assume the events in question occurred as reported, as these theists do not currently acknowledge a valid pattern of direct divine intervention of this sort in our world.

This is not to say that observing/experiencing a given event – for example, the immediate disappearance of a parent's cancerous growth at a healing service – might not for a given theist lead this person to affirm a divine action pattern not previously acknowledged. However, I see this as the rare exception to the rule and so remain convinced that, for most theists, a necessary condition for labeling an event a miracle is that it be an instantiation of a recognized divine action pattern. And if this is so, since acceptable patterns differ from theist to theist, it should not be surprising that the types of events that will, in principle, be considered miraculous also differ from theist to theist.

3.3   Do Miracles Occur

Have any miracles, though, actually occurred? This question continues to generate significant philosophical discussion. And no purported miracle continues to receive more attention than the resurrection of Jesus.

Let's first consider the Resurrection as a historical event. Or, as Keith Parsons (2016) frames the question, "Does the balance of the historical evidence favor the Christian account, i.e., is the bodily resurrection of Jesus of Nazareth clearly the best explanation, when judged by the accepted standards of historical research, of the acknowledged events that occurred soon after his crucifixion?" Even this seemingly straightforward question, as Lidija Novakovic (2016: 156) notes, surfaces the continuing methodological debate between those who "insist that God's ability to intervene in the created world should not be excluded from the historian's world-view" and those who maintain just as strongly that it should be excluded.

Throughout this Element, I have attempted to draw and defend a clear distinction between an alleged miracle as a reported event and as a direct act of God. It should not be surprising, therefore, that I side with those who want to make a clear distinction between whether Jesus rose from the dead and whether, if so, this was the result of direct divine intervention in our world. Accordingly, the historical question as we will consider it is this: Assuming an agnostic stance on the questions of whether God exists and if so can intervene directly in earthly affairs, what does the historical evidence lead us to conclude about whether a man named Jesus died, was buried, and then came back to life?

Even if we assume that Jesus did live, was crucified, and buried, there remains considerable difference of opinion on the strength of the historical evidence for the claim that Jesus rose from the dead. Although details differ, the general evidential case for the resurrection of Jesus as I see it can be summarized as follows (Davis, 1984; Habermas, 1987; Novakovic, 2016).

Although New Testament accounts of the Resurrection differ (and even contradict each other on specific details), the biblical record uniformly claims that Jesus died, was buried, and then rose from the dead. Moreover, the fact that we are told that women discovered the tomb is a strong argument for the historicity of the Resurrection since as Novakovic (2016: 134) notes, "female testimony had little weight in the first-century Jewish world." Furthermore, there is no good reason to believe that the disciples were hallucinating (were simply imagining things that were not actually occurring) as none of the normal causes for hallucination – mass hysteria, food or sleep deprivation, or drugs – appears to have been present. Nor do we have any good reason to believe that the disciples were lying, as their lives were so radically changed by this belief that many were willing to die rather than denounce their faith. Finally, there was no conclusive refutation of Jesus' resurrection by Jewish authorities – for example, they didn't produce the body – although they had the power and motivation to do so. So we can rightly conclude, in the words of Gary Habermas (1987: 29), that while there are other possible interpretations of the historical evidence, "Jesus' literal Resurrection from the dead . . . is the best explanation for the facts."

Not surprisingly, many nontheists and some theists contend that such evidence is not compelling (Martin, 1991; Keller, 1988; Parsons, 2016). Again, details differ, but the essence of their critique seems to be the following.

While it may well be that many historians agree that Jesus lived and died by crucifixion, it is not at all clear that the disciples or the very early church actually believed that Jesus had risen from the dead and appeared to many of his followers. In fact, it is most reasonable to believe that the resurrection story entered the Christian tradition well after its inception. Parsons (2016) tells us, for example, that

> of the earliest NT writings, Mark and the Pauline epistles, the first says nothing about the postmortem "appearances" and the latter is wholly lacking in detail. However, the accounts written decades later offer engaging and detailed accounts. Information generally decays over time, so I take the silence of the early accounts and the richness of the later ones as *prima facie* evidence that these stories were confabulated, concocted, or at least greatly embellished in the interim.

Others such as Reginald Fuller (1980) believe we are simply not in an evidential position to say when this story became a key component of faith.

Second, we do not have much independent, objective evidence for the gospel accounts of the resurrection. And even within the gospel accounts, the inconsistencies among the gospels on such issues as which women were present, who was in the tomb, what the women did after their discovery, and how the disciples reacted are not simply minor difficulties. Such inconsistencies place into serious doubt the historical reliability of the biblical texts.

Third, it may well be true that the disciples believed so firmly that Jesus rose from the dead that they were willing to die for their faith. However, this in no way makes the truth of the resurrection claim more probable as there are surely numerous examples of religious zealots – for example, the followers of Jim Jones or David Koresh – who gave their lives for what many, including many of those who believe in the resurrection, adamantly deny to be the truth. Furthermore, Parsons (2016) reminds us, even "sincere, honest people often make up stories without consciously fabricating them and with no intention to deceive. False stories spontaneously rise and quickly spread, especially when teller and audience are strongly motivated to believe them."

Fourth, even if we assume that the Jewish authorities were aware of the resurrection claims and weren't able to counter the resurrection claim by producing the body, the probability that an actual resurrection took place does not increase. It is just as plausible to believe that the Jewish authorities didn't have enough evidence for an objective refutation because there were no independent, unbiased eyewitnesses to the events in question or that the body had been stolen and hidden by the disciples.

Finally, it is important to remember that the burden of proof clearly lies with those who believe Jesus to have risen from the dead. Our human experience continues to confirm daily the undesirable but obvious fact: dead people stay dead. The historical evidence for any claim to the contrary must, therefore, be exceedingly strong. However, the relevant evidence is weak at best, especially if one does not build in theological (non-historic) presuppositions concerning God's existence and communication with humanity through sacred texts. Hence, we must conclude, critics maintain, that there simply exists no valid historical basis for maintaining that the resurrection of Jesus is an established fact (or even a reasonable probability).

Those who believe in the historicity of the resurrection or are simply not convinced by these challenges not surprisingly offer counters. They claim, for instance, that the gospel accounts of the resurrection, if properly interpreted, contain no significant contradictions. And the critics' contention that many sincere (but possibly misguided) individuals in addition to the disciples have died for what they believed to be the truth misses the point, they argue. It is the fact that the disciples were in a position to know whether Jesus came back to life that makes their perspective unique.

I agree that critics have not proved conclusively the claim that Jesus rose from the dead to be false. I also agree that supporters have not proved conclusively the resurrection claim to be true. Where does this leave us with respect to rational belief? Or, as Parsons (2016) frames one side of this question: given our understanding of the historical evidence, does belief in the Resurrection as a historical event remain a "rational, epistemically responsible belief for thoughtful, intelligent, educated Christians?" Moreover, the same can be asked in relation to critics. Given our understanding of the evidence, does their belief that the Resurrection did not occur remain a rational, epistemically responsible position?

The answer is clear for some on both sides of the issue. Michael Martin and Antony Flew believe the historical evidence to be so weak that, in Martin's (1991: 96) words, a "rational person should disbelieve the claim that Jesus was resurrected from the dead." On the other hand, Gary Habermas believes the historical evidence for the resurrection of Jesus to be so strong that no sincere, knowledgeable person can rationally deny that this event actually occurred.

Stephen Davis (1985) offers us a middle ground, based on the distinction highlighted in this Element between simply defending one's right to hold a belief and arguing that no one can rationally disagree. Davis believes personally that the historical evidence, considered alone, clearly supports the resurrection of Jesus. He denies, however, that sincere, knowledgeable individuals cannot justifiably disagree. Individuals' perspectives on whether Jesus actually rose from the dead ultimately come down to their basic worldview – their basic perspective on the nature of reality. Since both supernaturalism and naturalism can be held by rational people, differing rational perspectives on the historicity of the event in question must also be allowed.[10]

Michel Sarot (2014) offers us a similar perspective. It's true, he acknowledges, that the methods of historical-critical science cannot establish that the resurrection of Jesus did or did not really occur. However, theists can justifiably reject the contention that only those events that can be established by the historical-critical science can rightly be said to have occurred since theists can justifiably affirm the existence of a God who intervenes in our world in ways that override or circumvent the natural order. Accordingly, the theist can justifiably maintain that "the Resurrection and ... other miracles really took place. They are facts but not historical facts. They took place ... but one needs the eyes of faith to see it."

Not surprisingly, I hold with Davis and Sarot that in the absence of any objective, non–question-begging arguments to the contrary by those on either side, those on both sides remain rational in affirming their positions on the Resurrection as a historical event.

There remains, though, another important question to consider: even if we grant that Jesus did die and then came back to life, do we have any reason to believe he was raised from the dead by God, and thus, that the Resurrection was indeed a miracle? Habermas and Davis are among those who believe personally that the probability that such an event could be explained without reference to direct divine intervention is very low. In fact, Habermas (1987: 39–42) seems to believe that when the evidence for the Resurrection is conjoined "with the claims of Jesus" – Jesus' claim, for instance, that he was uniquely related to God or that the Resurrection would verify this fact – the denial of direct divine activity in this case borders on irrationality. Davis does not go this far. While he

---

[10] A somewhat analogous line of reasoning is offered by J. Houston (1994).

questions whether someone can maintain that the Resurrection occurred and yet deny divine intervention, he holds that naturalists can rationally deny the historicity of this event, in which case, of course, no explanation is needed.

Critics such as Martin (1991) reject the supernaturalist perspective. They argue that even if one grants that the resurrection of Jesus occurred, one can rationally deny that it was brought about by God (is a miracle) since it is just as plausible that this unusual event was the result of natural laws not yet discovered or fully understood or that this event was simply uncaused by either natural or supernatural means.

I agree with Davis at this point. As I see it, the occurrence of no event itself could require all rational individuals to acknowledge a divine causal explanation as Habermas maintains. On the other hand, the fact that there is a plausible natural explanation for an event doesn't mean that affirming a divine causal explanation can be rejected, as Martin would have us believe. Since I believe that theists can justifiably affirm the existence of a God who at times circumvents or overrides the natural order, I believe that theists can justifiably believe that the Resurrection not only occurred but was the result of divine intervention. However, it is equally justifiable for nontheists, or those theists who have reason to believe God did not or cannot intervene, to deny divine intervention as a causal factor, even if they were to admit the event occurred.

4 Theological Issues

The primary purpose of this Section is to discuss important issues that arise when considering the nature and role of evil and prayer in religious belief systems that posit a God who can intervene miraculously in earthly affairs. To best understand and engage profitably in discussion of these issues, we first need to distinguish between two basic perspectives on the nature and efficacy of God's power. Both of these understandings of God's power vis-à-vis the natural world allow for the type of direct divine intervention required for miracles. They differ significantly, however, on the question of how God's power is related to human freedom, and these differences have significant implications for how proponents of these perspectives understand the relationship among evil, prayer, and miracle.

As was first noted in Section 2, proponents of Theological Determinism maintain that God is all-controlling. Humans are free and responsible for their actions, but all and only that which God has determined (decreed) should happen does happen. This does not mean of course that God likes all that occurs. Not everything that occurs in the world is inherently desirable or pleasing to God. However, everything that occurs has been decreed by God as part of a perfect plan for our world and is thus instrumentally necessary, although we will quite likely never in this life be in a position to understand how this could be so. Accordingly, God never intervenes directly in earthly affairs to fix a problem or right a wrong in the sense that the world would have been better off if these problems or wrongs had never existed in the first place. Rather, both the problems and wrongs we experience, along with any and all divine interventions to address them, were from the beginning necessary components in God's perfect plan for this best of all possible worlds (Basinger, 1996).

Proponents of what is most often labelled Freewill Theism maintain that God possesses the same type and capacity of power as that of the God of Theological Determinism and thus could be all-controlling. Moreover, God does at times use this power to intervene unilaterally in our world. God, for instance, created the world ex nihilo and can and does occasionally override the natural order and/or human freedom to ensure a desired outcome – for example, to fix problems and right wrongs. However, to the extent that God grants us meaningful freedom, God has voluntarily given up control over what will occur as a result. Accordingly, there is inherent risk in this world. Not all that occurs is in keeping with the divine will. Some (much) of what occurs is not even instrumentally necessary. The world would have been better off without it (Basinger, 1996: 32–36).

4.1   Miracle and Evil

Let's first consider key issues related to miracle and evil. Christine Overall is probably the best-known proponent of the contention that if miracles are understood to be violations or circumventions of the natural order, their occurrence would actually count against God's existence.

First, Overall points out (2003b: 151), the occurrence of such miracles would undermine the standard teleological (design) argument for God's existence:

> Some philosophers and theologians have urged us to consider the supposed order, regularity, and harmony of the universe as evidence of the existence of a benign and omnipotent god. But if order, regularity, and harmony constitute evidence for God, then miracles cannot *also* be accepted as evidence for his existence, for they are, to follow the metaphor, dissonances in the harmony, holes in the patterned fabric of the universe. Hence, a Christian believer cannot have it both ways.

This argument presupposes that a theist cannot consistently maintain both that the regularity and order in nature count as evidence for God's existence and that exceptions to this regularity and order can also count as evidence for God's existence. If a given theist were assuming fully natural causation in both cases, then there might here be some sort of consistency problem. However, as we have repeatedly seen in other Sections, many theists distinguish clearly between two differing types of causation in relation to our world: fully natural and at least partially non-natural. Theists proposing versions of the teleological argument are claiming that the order and regularity in the natural order, when running on its own apart from any direct divine intervention, does point to a purposeful intelligent creator. Many of these same theists, though, also want to claim that the creator of the natural order – the creator of the natural causal laws governing what will occur naturally – does at times intervene in this natural order to bring about events that are counterinstances to what nature itself would cause to occur and that this also evidences God's existence. Of course, there are many who will maintain that neither argument is successful. However, I fail to see any inherent inconsistency in affirming both arguments as long as the differing form of causation in each is clearly understood. This is the case whether the theists in question are Theological Determinists, who believe all interventions (circumventions or overridings of the natural order) were decreed as necessary components in the best of all possible worlds, or Freewill Theists, who allow that God can intervene in response to what is occurring naturally.

Second, Overall makes a related argument that the occurrence of miracles "would interfere with the attempt to understand the structure and regularities of reality" (2006: 356) in the sense that the occurrence of miracles would be

> misleading to human beings who, as knowledge-seekers, attempt to understand the world by discerning regularities and patterns in it. The extreme rarity of miracles and the difficulties and controversies in identifying them are an impediment to the growth of scientific and philosophical comprehension. A benevolent God would not mislead his people (2003b: 150).

Or, as Overall (2014: 605) has stated this point more recently,

> The alleged miracles would ... not be susceptible to *any* sort of naturalistic understanding and explanation by human beings. This inaccessibility would be an epistemic evil because it would be a *permanent* exception to all human knowledge about our reality. (emphasis added)

The main problem here, as I see it, is that Overall does not grant that it is conceptually possible to assume the regularity of the natural order for functional purposes while acknowledging the possibility of an overriding or circumvention of this natural order. If we maintain – as I argued in Section 2 we should – that science must always assume that there could be a fully natural explanation for any event type even if we cannot offer one at present, then the fact that there might actually be some event tokens that don't actually have fully natural explanations will not impede scientific study. In fact, as McGrew (2016) points out, there is little evidence it has done so.

Overall's third challenge, however, is one of a set of serious concerns that focus not on the conceptual or epistemological status of the miraculous but, rather, on the implications of God's alleged miraculous activity for God's moral nature.

The key problem, as Overall (2014: 607) sees it, is the morally indefensible scope and number of the miracles purported done by God:

> When alleged miracles purport to make a major change (as in raising Lazarus from the dead), *they solve the problems of only a select few, ignoring almost all of the unmet needs, deliberate cruelty, and enormous suffering in both human and non-human beings.* (emphasis added)

Overall actually touches on two related concerns here. One focuses on the question of why a good God who can intervene to help those in need (and per hypothesis has done so) does not do so more frequently. As process theist David Griffin (Griffin, Cobb, & Schroeder, 1981: 193) states this concern: why would a good God who can unilaterally intervene not do so more frequently "in order to prevent particularly horrendous evils?"

Matthew McCormick (2012: 182–83) agrees: "Every case where someone claims that her prayers led to her rapid recovery from terminal cancer, or that his piety helped bring back a loved one safe from the fighting in a war zone," he argues, "shines a light on all the other cases of suffering that went unabated despite heartfelt prayers, decent lives, and fervent piety." And this, he concludes, counts heavily against attributing omnibenevolence to the source.

The other, related concern raised by Overall focuses on the question of why the number of divine interventions that do allegedly take place, even if justifiably limited in number, do not occur in a fairer, more morally even fashion.

The Bible states not only that God intervened to raise individuals from the dead and heal the sick but also that Jesus multiplied the two loaves and fishes so they wouldn't be hungry. Theists today sometimes talk about God intervening not only to cure people of cancer but also to alleviate back problems or severe headaches. However, if God is in fact limited in the number of miracles that can be performed, then why don't we see God using these limited interventive opportunities to respond to the truly horrendous evils we face? Taking away back pain is fine, but the "evil" being countered in this case is clearly not equivalent to the evil being experienced by those large numbers of innocent children being brutally tortured and killed each day.

The Theological Determinist has a ready response to such challenges to God's moral nature. While it may appear from our human perspective that a good God who can intervene beneficially would do so more often and fairly, this is, per hypothesis, the best of all possible worlds. So we must assume that the number, types, and distribution of divine interventions are exactly as they need to be. Any more or less would make this less than God's perfect creation.

While this type of response is not normally convincing to those who don't share the assumptions of Theological Determinism, I know of no objective, non–question-begging arguments by which it can be demonstrated that such a response cannot justifiably be affirmed.

The response of the Freewill Theist to these two related moral challenges is significantly different from that of the Theological Determinist. Freewill Theists, like most theists, acknowledge the reality of some "necessary" evil – that is, evil that is a necessary condition for the actualization of some acknowledged good. However, as noted previously, Freewill Theists deny that God can both grant us meaningful freedom – the ability to bring about both good and evil – and also unilaterally control the decision-making process in such a way that we will always make the exact decisions God would have us make, even though we have, per hypothesis, the power to do so. That is, Freewill Theists believe that human decision-making is capable of producing unavoidable gratuitous evil – instances of evil that have no inherent or instrumental value but are unavoidable byproducts of the actualization of God's desire for individuals to exercise meaningful freedom. Accordingly, since Freewill Theists believe that God did choose to create a world containing individuals who possess significant freedom, they acknowledge that this world may well contain unavoidable gratuitous moral evil as well as necessary evil (Basinger, 1996).

But what of natural evil? How can such evil be explained in terms of meaningful human freedom? One common response is that meaningful free choice is only possible in a world with a predictable natural order that allows individuals to assume that certain states of affairs will follow from certain choices. For instance, our choices to run or not run or jump or not jump in a given situation are based on our assumption that gravity is a constant. But the same constant state of gravity that makes the choice to walk along a cliff possible can also bring about serious harm or death to someone who falls off the cliff.

Moreover, Freewill Theists deny that God had (has) knowledge of any world (or type of world) that could have been initiated (could be initiated now) that would better satisfy the divine creative goals.[11] That is, they believe that since God is good, God would have created a world in which meaningful freedom results in the number, types, and distribution of moral and natural evil we experience only if such a world contains a net balance of good that is greater than that which would exist in any other actualizable world that contained the possibility of both moral good and evil. Or stated differently yet, Freewill Theists deny that this world contains any gratuitous moral or natural evil God could remove and yet allows. Thus, they conclude that the evil in this world is not incompatible with the existence of the perfectly good, all powerful being to whom they give allegiance, even if this world contains many states of affairs that are inherently undesirable (Hasker, 1989).

---

[11] Those who believe God possesses middle knowledge deny that God, before creation, had knowledge of any actualizable world that would have better satisfied God's creative goals. Those who believe God possesses only present knowledge or simple foreknowledge deny that God, since creation, has ever had such knowledge. See Section 2.

The Freewill Theist, of course, does not assume that such responses explain the number, types, and distribution of divine interventions related to evil in a way that will be satisfying to the nontheists or even some theists. But I know of no objective, non-question-begging basis for demonstrating that such responses are false or even unjustified – that is, cannot be affirmed by a rational person. And that is sufficient, I believe, to counter the claim that the fact that God does not, from the critic's perspective, miraculously intervene more frequently and/or fairly is a successful objective argument against God's goodness or existence.

A final moral concern moves the challenge away from ways in which a good God should intervene but does not to ways in which a good God should not have intervened but allegedly did. Specifically, the accusation is that God has intervened in ways that are themselves evil.

Frank Jankunis (2014: 588–89) asks us to consider, for example, God's actions in Numbers. In response to the complaints of Korah, Dathan, Abiram, and their 250 supporters, God causes the ground to split open under Dathan, Abiram, and Korah, swallowing them, their families, and possessions. God then sends fire to burn the remaining 250 supporters. While "one may be able to contextualize turning water into wine for the sake of a good part ... it is a good deal harder," Jankunis notes, "to contextualize spontaneous mass murder of religious adherents."

Or consider the biblical account of the killing of Midianite women and children found in Numbers 31. Moses has sent 12,000 Israelite soldiers to "exact vengeance on the Midianites." When he discovers that they have killed only the Midianite men and brought back approximately 100,000 women and children, he commands them to "kill all the boys, and kill every woman who has slept with a man, but save for yourselves every girl who has not slept with a man." The story then ends with the officers returning with an offering to God in thanks for the fact that they have not lost a single man in this successful effort.

While it appears that these soldiers – who had not only killed about 30,000 men but then chased down and killed about 65,000 woman and children before taking home their share of the 32,000 virgin girls – did not suffer pangs of moral conscience for their actions, few Christians or Jews today can understand how anyone, especially anyone living in relationship with and attempting to follow the teachings of the true God, could do such things with gratitude to God for the outcome (Basinger, 2011).

Finally, consider the situation of King David in 2nd Samuel. David has sinned, and in response, the "LORD sent a pestilence upon Israel from the morning even to the time appointed: and there died of the people from Dan even to Beersheba seventy thousand men." It appears from the text that David himself is questioning the fairness of this divine action when he speaks to the Lord, saying: "Lo, I have sinned, and I have done wickedly: but these sheep, what have they done?"

Theistic responses to this type of criticism normally fall into one of two categories. Some (both Freewill Theists and Theological Determinists) affirm or at least presuppose what is sometimes called the moral continuity thesis. This perspective assumes that our most fundamental moral intuitions concerning just behavior and/or what we are told in holy texts to be just behavior have their basis in God's moral nature; that is, presupposes that God does act, and that we are to act, in relation to the same basic understanding of just behavior.

Accordingly, those affirming this understanding of God's moral nature normally argue that while the types of situations in question may look unjust from our perspective, this is very likely not actually the case. If we understood all the relevant factors in each case, we would agree that God's action or inaction was just. In some cases, what seemed an arbitrary, unjust action might not actually have been so, given all the potential implications of this act of which God was aware at the time. In other cases, it's possible that the seemingly unjust divine action is actually inherently unjust, in and of itself, but was a necessary condition for a greater good of which we are not aware. Or as Jankunis (2014: 588) has recently summarized Robert Larmer's perspective on this point, "Any apparent bias and triviality of miracles can be accounted for in a morally satisfactory way by appeal to the specifics of each case and the broader context in which biblical miracles are said to have occurred." However, whether we can conceive of a reasonable explanation or not, we can be assured that God has in fact always actually acted in accordance with the same concept of just behavior that is causing the tension in question for us (Basinger, 1996).

The other type of response to this moral challenge – a version of the Divine Command tradition – holds that God is under no obligation to treat any individual in what we would consider a just, fair fashion. God can do what God wants for whatever reason God wants to do so. What God does is right simply because God does it. Christian proponents of this view often point to Romans 9: 16–22, where we read that just as potters can do with a lump of clay whatever they want for whatever reason, so too can God do what God wants with and to us as humans for God's own reasons.

Not surprisingly, those holding this perspective will not try to defend God's goodness against claims that God's direct interventions of the type in question are arbitrary and capacious by offering what might to humans seem plausible reasons for such divine behavior. Rather, given this perspective, there is, in fact, no problem related to God's moral nature to resolve. Once we come to understand that we cannot judge God's behavior by our basic human moral principles (even those principles found in scriptural texts telling us how we as humans ought to live), the question under consideration is no longer relevant.

Have Theological Determinists and Freewill Theists offered us adequate responses to this third moral challenge? This depends on the exact nature of the question being asked. If the question is whether all rational individuals must accept these responses as reasonable or remotely plausible replies to what appears to be morally questionable direct divine intervention in our world, including allegedly miraculous direct intervention, the answer is obviously no. However, if the question is whether a rational person can accept these responses as adequate, I think the answer is yes. These responses don't strike me as self-contradictory or inconsistent with the belief that God exists and is good. Nor am I aware of any objective, non–question-begging evidence for the claim that such responses are ad hoc, improbable, implausible, or even just morally offensive. So, I believe they can justifiably be affirmed by the relevant theists as adequate responses to the challenge in question.

However, one final comment is necessary. It's important to note that at least two general tensions remain, even if responses to the challenges above do preserve justified belief. First, for the Freewill Theist, the acknowledged frequency of gratuitous (undesired but unavoidable) evil and the expected frequency of miraculous direct divine intervention stand in an inverse relationship. The more Freewill Theists respond to specific instances of evil by claiming that God cannot remove them because of the self-limitation imposed in a moral universe containing free choice, the less reason they have to expect beneficial (miraculous) intervention in any specific situation. Second, the more Freewill Theists or Theological Determinists attempt to resolve the concerns in question by claiming that "God's ways are above our ways," the less able they will be to predict or recognize when and where any such miraculous divine intervention might occur.

4.2 Miracle and Petitionary Prayer

We'll move now to key issues related to miracle and petitionary prayer. As noted earlier, one key way in which discussions of miracle and prayer can intersect is around the role humans can play in bringing about miracles. There are two purportedly efficacious aspects of petitionary prayer that don't come into play here. Specifically, we will not concern ourselves with the claim that petitionary prayer can have a positive effect on the petitioner – for example, that a petitioner may experience psychological benefit by sharing a request with a being (God) who it is believed can help. Nor will we concern ourselves with the claim that petitionary prayer can have a positive impact on individuals who know that prayers are being offered on their behalf – for example, that the petitionee may experience gratitude or peace.

The question on which we will focus is the one raised first in Section 2:

> Does God sometimes directly intervene in response to a request to bring about a "miraculous" event that (1) God desired to occur and was able to ensure would occur but that (2) would not have occurred – God would not have intervened to bring about – if the request had not been made?

Or stated in a form better suited for our purpose, can a theist who believes that God is able to intervene directly in earthly affairs in ways that circumvent or override the natural order maintain justifiably that humans can, at least in principle, play a necessary casual role in some instances of such divine activity?

As we saw in Section 2, the Theological Determinist cannot respond affirmatively. God may well have decided that human petitioning would be a component in the sequence of events leading to a divine intervention. However, since the God of Theological Determinism can control free human choice, it can never be the case that a human decision outside of God's control is a necessary determining factor in whether God will act miraculously in our world.

On the other hand, Freewill Theists can answer this question affirmatively. Since the God of Freewill Theism can unilaterally intervene but cannot unilaterally control free human choice, freely offered petitionary prayer can, in principle, be a necessary determining factor in miraculous divine intervention.

However, that this is so raises for Freewill Theism a serious moral concern (Basinger 1983; Basinger, 1995). If God is able to intervene in a given situation – that is, if the limits on God's ability to intervene in a world containing meaningful human freedom do not restrict God from intervening in a given situation – and God desired to intervene in this situation – that is, if to do so is in keeping with what God believes is the best outcome in this situation – then why would a good God ever wait to intervene miraculously until requested to do so? Why, for instance, if God is able to heal someone who has cancer and this is something God desires to occur, would God ever wait until petitioned by someone to miraculously intervene?

I'll briefly state and critique some standard responses offered by Freewill Theists. According to Eleonore Stump (1979), God loves us and wants to be loved freely in return. However, a meaningful relationship between an infinite creator and finite creatures like us – who possess significant freedom – can only be developed and maintained if God does not dominate or spoil us, which would occur if God always automatically gave us all that we need or brought it about that things turned out for the best. One way God can avoid such domination or spoiling is for God to refrain from intervening in our lives upon occasion until we request divine assistance.

Michael Murray and Kurt Meyers offer a similar response (Murray & Meyers, 1994). When that which a person desires comes to her as the result of her own human efforts, it is easy for this person to believe she is the master of her own fate. But if God withholds that which God would like a person to receive at times until she asks for it, she is then forced "to consider that the goods that accrue to her do so ultimately because of forces beyond human control." That is, she is "forcefully reminded that she is directly dependent on God for her provisions in life ... that God is the ultimate source of all goods" (Murray & Meyers, 1994: 314). It is not necessary for God to "make provision of all goods hang on creaturely petition in order to achieve the good of preserving creatures from idolatry." These occasions need only "be frequent enough to achieve" the desired end (Murray & Meyers, 1994: 317).

As I have argued in another context, this type of response seems to me inadequate (Basinger, 1995). Let us define as a basic human need that which is required to achieve the basic levels of physical and mental health without which life is not possible or the quality of life is greatly diminished. Included here might be such things as enough food/shelter to live or develop as one should, enough relational activity to develop socially, or the ability to avoid or overcome life-threatening challenges. And let us define as a discretionary human need that which adds to the quality of life for a self-sufficient, healthy person – for example, a new, well-running car, time off work to replenish one's spirits, enough money to buy favorite records, etc.

It seems reasonable to maintain that God might refrain from intervening to meet discretionary needs until requested so as not to spoil/dominate us or to make us more aware of the beneficial role God plays in our lives. However, for God to refrain from intervening until petitioned makes much less sense in terms of basic needs – for example, the need for sufficient food and shelter to live, the need for a single mother to overcome disease so she can be there for her children, etc. If we assume the moral continuity thesis – that is, if the moral principles that guide God's action and are to guide ours are the same because they both have their origin in God's moral nature – then for God to refrain from intervening in relation to such basic needs until requested so as not to spoil/dominate us or make us more aware of his care for us appears unjustified at best.

One possible rejoinder, Murray and Meyers note (Murray & Meyers, 1994), is to maintain that God only refrains from acting until requested with respect to discretionary needs. However, this would seem to minimize the perceived value of prayer for those theists (I think the majority) who believe that petitionary prayer is of most value in relation to basic needs, especially needs met by God's miraculous circumvention or overriding of the natural order.

Murray and Meyers offer us another possible reason for why the God of Freewill Theism might wait to intervene until requested, a line of reasoning that opens the door to a fruitful epistemological discussion on our ability to identify miracles, even if they do occur.

It is sometimes the case, they note, human parents use the opportunity to respond to their children's petitions to "teach their children what is right and important and what is not" (Murray & Meyers, 1994: 318). When they refrain from granting certain requests, "the parents indicate to the child that there are certain things that, for various reasons, are not in their interests, contrary to the child's belief." On the other hand, by granting certain requests they have "the opportunity to foster important virtues in the child" (Murray & Meyers, 1994: 318).

This same basic principle, Murray and Meyers maintain (1994: 319), can also hold for believers and their heavenly parent. When believers request something from God and the request is granted, they have not only had a need fulfilled, they also have continued the process of learning the types of desires that are in accordance with God's will. Similarly, when believers petition God and their request in not granted, they are able to learn that their desires are not in accordance with God's will. And by learning in this fashion about God's will, believers "may in turn learn to become more righteous, and thus better conformed to the image of God."

This line of reasoning seems plausible at the human level. Complications arise, though, when we consider whether answered or unanswered prayer can exemplify God's values for a Freewill Theist. Children can learn about their parents' values by responses to requests only if they are clearly aware of the fact that their parents are the ones who are giving to (or withholding from) them that which they have requested and that their parents' doing so is an accurate indication of their moral assessment of that which the children desire. In similar fashion, believers can learn about God's values from that which occurs after their petitions only to the extent that they can have some degree of certainty that they are receiving (or not receiving) what they have requested because of a decision made by God and that this decision was made primarily because their request was consistent (or inconsistent) with God's values.

Can a Freewill Theist, though, have access to such information? Let's first consider unfulfilled requests. Given any theistic perspective, it's possible that a believer didn't receive what was requested because the request was not in keeping with God's values. However, given any theistic perspective, it is equally possible to assume that although what was requested was perfectly compatible with God's moral nature, God decided for some other reason –

for instance, for the overall good of the petitioner or someone else – not to grant the request (at least at this time).

Moreover, Freewill Theists believe that God's decision to create a world in which individuals exercise meaningful freedom does in fact significantly (self) limit God's ability to intervene in earthly affairs. Accordingly, for these theists, a third, equal possibility always exists: while the request was in keeping with God's moral values, God was not able to intervene in this case given the parameters of the self-limitation of granting humans freedom.

Hence, since I do not believe Freewill Theists to be in a position, even in principle, to determine which of these three equally possible options is in fact the one applicable in any given case, I see no justifiable basis for Freewill Theists to conclude solely or primarily on the basis of the fact that they did not receive that which was requested that what they requested was most likely not consistent with God's values.

What, though, of those cases in which a theist has received what was requested – for example, experienced a complete remission from terminal cancer following a request to God for healing? Could it then be most reasonable for a theist to assume that God was the source of the desired action (and thus that the request was consistent with God's values)? The answer is yes, if we make an assumption. We are clearly justified at the human level in believing that a person has responded affirmatively to a request when we already possess good reasons for believing that this person is likely to respond in this manner, and there exists no equally plausible reason to think this wasn't what occurred in this case.

Likewise, it seems to me that if believers who have received what was requested from God already possess a reasonable basis for maintaining that God answers prayers of the type in question affirmatively, and these believers are aware of no plausible reason for believing either that God would not do so in their specific case or that the desired state of affairs was about to occur anyway, then they are justified in assuming that their prayer was answered by God. However, if believers must possess a reasonable basis for believing that God answers prayers of the relevant type before they can justifiably attribute any specific response to God, then they already know that their request is compatible with God's values and, accordingly, the fact that their specific request has been granted can teach them nothing new about how God would have us live.

Hence, it should not be surprising that I do not consider the suggestions that God at times withholds provisions so as not to spoil us and/or help us learn divine values (and hence become more like God) to be very plausible responses to the challenge to God's moral nature in question. This is not to say, of course, that there might not be a justifiable reason for God to withhold provision until requested. My argument is only that none of the reasons offered to date appear to me adequate.

What are the key takeaways here for our discussion of miracles? Of course, it doesn't follow from our discussion of petitionary prayer that miracles can't occur or that a theist cannot justifiably maintain that God has intervened in a miraculous manner. But there is a strong theistic tradition (that of Freewill Theism whether it is labeled that or not) that maintains (1) that humans can meaningfully contribute to when and how God miraculously intervenes through petitionary prayer and that (2) we can gain some insight about God and how God would have us live by observing the responses to such prayers.

I've argued that (1), it is difficult to see how a benevolent Freewill God could justifiably wait to intervene until requested in the cases that matter most to Freewill Theists – in situations where someone's basic needs are in jeopardy. And (2), it is difficult to see how the Freewill Theist can learn anything new about God's values – what God is like or how God would have us live – by observing whether our prayers for God's interventive activity are answered, since the Freewill Theist isn't in a position to read from what occurs in response to prayer anything definitive about God's participation and intention in relation to the state of affairs in question that isn't already known.

5 Concluding Comments

As this Element illustrates, analytic philosophy's interest in the miraculous continues unabated. Many, if not most, of the same basic issues discussed fifty years ago remain. Is the concept of a violation of a natural law coherent? Under what conditions, if any, is it justifiable to accept the report of a counterinstance to our current set of natural laws as accurate? Are there any conditions under which it would be most rational for all individuals to grant that an event acknowledged as having occurred and currently inexplicable naturally is, in fact, permanently inexplicable naturally? Are there any conceivable scenarios in which the search for the cause of a currently inexplicable event acknowledged to have occurred would require all rational individuals to also acknowledge that this event had in part a supernatural cause?

More recently, philosophers have shown increasing interest in the questions concerning the relationship between miracle and evil that arise when we start considering why a God who can and does intervene in earthly affairs to help those in need does not do so in a more frequent and seemingly fairer manner. Philosophers have also, as I see it, been less inclined recently to argue for the truth of a position and more inclined to consider what can be justifiably believed (at times by those on both sides of an issue).

Moreover, the fact that the miraculous is of existential as well as theoretical interest to many ensures, I think, that philosophical analysis of the concept of miracle will continue for the foreseeable future. It is my hope this brief overview of the current state of the discussion around these enduring and new issues will contribute to such an ongoing assessment.

References

American Heritage Dictionary. (2000). Boston: Houghton Mifflin.

Adams, R. (1992). Miracles, Laws and Natural Causation (II). *Proceedings of the Aristotelian Society, Supplementary Volume,* 60, pp. 207–24.

Aquinas, T. *SCG*3.103; *ST* 1.110, art. 4.

Boden, M. (1969). Miracles and Scientific Explanation. *Ratio,* 11, pp. 137–44.

Basinger, D. (1983). Why Petition an Omnipotent, Omniscient, Wholly Good God? *Religious Studies,* 19(1), pp. 25–41.

Basinger, D. (1987). Miracles and Natural Explanation. *Sophia,* 26(3), pp. 22–26.

Basinger, D. (1988). *Divine Power in Process Theism: A Philosophical Critique.* Albany: State University of New York Press.

Basinger, D. (1995). Petitionary Prayer: A response to Murray and Meyers. *Religious Studies,* 31(4), pp. 475–84.

Basinger, D. (1996). *The Case for Freewill Theism.* Downers Grove, IL: InterVarsity Press.

Basinger, D. (2002). *Religious Diversity: A Philosophical Assessment.* Burlington, VT: Ashgate.

Basinger, D. (2011). Religious Belief Formation: A Kantian Approach Informed by Science. In Oord, T., Zimmerman, D., and Hasker, W., eds., *God in an Open Universe: Science, Metaphysics, and Open Theism.* Eugene,OR: Pickwick Press, pp. 57–60.

Basinger, D. (2013). Introduction to Open Theism. In Diller, J. and Kasher, A., eds., *Models of God and of Other Ultimate Realities.* Springer, Netherlands, pp. 263–75.

Basinger, D. and Basinger, R. (1986). *Philosophy and Miracle: The Contemporary Debate.* Lewiston, NY: Edwin Mellen Press.

Burgess, M., McGee, G., and Alexander, P., eds. (1988). *Dictionary of Pentecostal and Charismatic Movements.* Grand Rapids, MI: Zondervan.

Bylica, P. (2015). Levels of Analysis in Philosophy, Religion, and Science. *Zygon,* 50(2), 304–29.

Clarke, S. (1997). When to Believe in Miracles. *American Philosophical Quarterly,* 34(1), pp. 95–101.

Cobb, J. and Griffin, D. (1976). *Process Theology: An Introductory Exposition.* Louisville: Westminster Press.

Corner, D. (2017). Miracles. The Internet Encyclopedia of Philosophy, ISSN 2161-0002, http://www.iep.utm.edu/October 15, 2017.

Corner, D. (2007). *The Philosophy of Miracles.* New York: Continuum.

Davis, S. (1984). Is it Possible to Know that Jesus was Raised from the Dead? *Faith and Philosophy,* 1(2), pp. 147–59.

Davis, S. (1985). Naturalism and the Resurrection: A Reply to Habermas. *Faith and Philosophy,* 2(3), pp. 303–08.

Davis, S. (1990). Doubting the Resurrection: A Reply to James A. Keller. *Faith and Philosophy,* 7(1), pp. 99–111.

Dawkins, R. (2006). *The God Delusion.* Boston: Houghton Mifflin.

Drange, T. (1998). Science and Miracle. The Secular Web, http://www.infidels.org/library/modern/theodore_drange/miracles.html.

Evans, C. S. (1985). *Philosophy of Religion: Thinking about Faith (Contours of Christian Philosophy).* Downers Grove, IL: Inter-Varsity Press.

Flew, A. (1967). Miracles. *Encyclopedia of Philosophy,* vol. 5. New York: Macmillan and Free Press.

Flew, A. (1976). Parapsychology Revisited: Laws, Miracles and Repeatability. *The Humanist,* 36, pp. 28–30.

Fuller, R. (1980). *The Formation of the Resurrection Narratives,* rev. ed. Philadelphia: Fortress Press.

Griffin, D., Cobb, J., and Schroeder, W., eds. (1981). *Process Philosophy and Social Thought.* Chicago: Chicago Center for the Scientific Study of Religion.

Habermas, G. (author), Miethe, T. (ed.), Flew, A. (contributor). (1987). *Did Jesus Rise from the Dead? The Resurrection Debate.* San Francisco: Harper & Row.

Hájek, A. (2008). Are Miracles Chimerical? In Kvanvig, J., ed., *Oxford Studies in Philosophy of Religion,* vol. 1. Oxford: Oxford University Press, pp. 82–104.

Hasker, W. (1989). *God, Time and Knowledge.* Ithaca, NY: Cornell University Press.

Hick, J. (1973). *God and the Universe of Faiths.* Oxford: Oneworld Publications Ltd.

Holland, R. F. (1965). The Miraculous. *American Philosophical Quarterly,* 2(1), pp. 43–51.

Houston, J. (1994). *Reported Miracles.* Cambridge: Cambridge University Press.

Jacobs, L. (n.d.). Jewish View on Miracles. *My Jewish Learning*, www.myjewishlearning.com/article/jewish-views-on-miracles/.

Jankunis, F. (2014). Overall and Larmer on Miracles as Evidence for the Existence of God. *Dialogue*, 53(4), 585–99.

Jantzen, G. (1979). Hume on Miracles, History and Politics. *Christian Scholar's Review*, 8(4), pp. 318–25.

Keller, J. (1988). Contemporary Christian Doubts about the Resurrection. *Faith and Philosophy*, 5(1), pp. 40–60.

Kriger, P. (n.d.). What Do the World's Religions Say about Miracles? *National Geographic*, http://channel.nationalgeographic.com/the-story-of-god-with-morgan-freeman/articles/what-do-the-worlds-religions-say-about-miracles/.

Larmer, R. (1984). Miracles and Criteria. *Sophia*, 23(1), pp.4–10.

Larmer, R. (1988). *Water into Wine: An Investigation of the Concept of Miracle*. Montreal: McGill-Queen's University Press.

Larmer, R. (1994). Miracles, Evidence and Theism: A Further Apologia. *Sophia*, 33(1), pp. 51–57.

Levine, M. (2005). Miracles. Stanford *Encyclopedia of Philosophy*, https://plato.stanford.edu/archives/fall2010/entries/miracles/.

Luck, M. (2016). Defining Miracles: Direct vs. Indirect Causation. *Philosophy Compass*, 11(5), pp. 267–76.

Mackie, J. L. (1982). *The Miracle of Theism*. Oxford: Oxford University Press.

Martin, M. (1991). *The Case against Christianity*. Philadelphia: Temple University Press.

McCormick, M. (2012). *Atheism and the Case against Christ*. Amherst, NY: Prometheus Books, pp. 182–83.

McGrew, T. (2016). Miracles. *The Stanford Encyclopedia of Philosophy, Zalta, E., ed.*, https://plato.stanford.edu/archives/win2016/entries/miracles/.

McKinnon, A. (1967)."Miracle" and "Paradox." *American Philosophical Quarterly*, 4(4), pp. 308–14.

Midrash *Genesis Rabbah* 5:45; Midrash *Exodus Rabbah* 21:6; and Ethics of the Fathers/Pirkei Avot 5: 6.

Murray, M. and Meyers, K. (1994). Ask and It Will Be Given to You. *Religious Studies* 30(3), pp. 311–30.

Novakovic, L. (2016). *Resurrection: A Guide for the Perplexed*. London/New York: Bloomsbury T&T Clark.

Overall, C. (2003a). Miracles and Larmer. *Dialogue*, 42, pp. 123–35.

Overall, C. (2003b). Miracles as Evidence against the Existence of God. In Martin, M. and Monnier, R., eds., *The Impossibility of God*. Amherst, NY: Prometheus Books, pp. 147–53.

Overall, C. (2006). Miracles, Evidence, Evil, and God: A Twenty-Year Debate. *Dialogue*, 45(2), pp. 355–66.

Overall, C. (2014). Reply to "Overall and Larmer on Miracles as Evidence for the Existence of God." *Dialogue*, 53(4), pp. 601–09.

Parsons, K. (2016). Response to Stephen T. Davis on Resurrection and Hallucination. *The Secular Outpost*, http://www.patheos.com/blogs/secularoutpost/2016/02/19/response-to-stephen-t-davis-on-resurrection-and-hallucination/#ovcfmXAr6WUeyGSQ.99.

Plantinga, A. (1979). The Probabilistic Argument from Evil. *Philosophical Studies*, 35(1), pp. 1–53.

Plantinga, A. (2000). *Warranted Christian Belief*. New York: Oxford University Press.

Polkinghorne, J. (1986). *The Interaction of Science and Theology*. London: SPCK.

Randi, J. (1987). *The Faith Healers*. Amherst, NY: Prometheus Books.

Sarot, M. (2014). The Ultimate Miracle?: The Historicity of the Resurrection of Jesus. *HTS Theological Studies*, 70(1), https://hts.org.za/index.php/HTS/article/view/2721

Scott, K. (n.d.). Reformed Epistemology. *The Internet Encyclopedia of Philosophy*, ISSN 2161–0002, http://www.iep.utm.edu/.

Stacey, A. (2014). What is a Miracle? *The Religion of Islam*, www.islamreligion.com/articles/5291/what-is-miracle/.

Stump, E. (1979). Petitionary Prayer. *American Philosophical Quarterly*, 16(2), pp. 86–91.

Swinburne, R. (1970). *The Concept of Miracle*. London: Macmillan.

van Inwagen, P. (2006). *The Problem of Evil*. New York: Oxford University Press.

Vicens, L. C. (2016). On the Natural Law Defense and the Disvalue of Ubiquitous Miracles. *International Journal for Philosophy of Religion*, 80 (1), pp. 33–42.

Printed in the United States
By Bookmasters